ANNA LIVIA PLURABELLE

The Making of a Chapter

EDITED WITH AN INTRODUCTION BY

Fred H. Higginson

THE UNIVERSITY OF MINNESOTA PRESS · MINNEAPOLIS

© Copyright 1939 by James Joyce

© Copyright 1960 by Harriet Weaver and F. Lionel Munro, as administrators c.t.a. of the Estate of James Joyce

© Copyright 1960 by the University of Minnesota

ALL RIGHTS RESERVED

Printed in the United States of America at the Lund Press, Inc., Minneapolis

Library of Congress Catalog Card Number: 60-10060

PUBLISHED IN GREAT BRITAIN, INDIA, AND PAKISTAN BY THE OXFORD UNIVERSITY PRESS, LONDON, BOMBAY, AND KARACHI, AND IN CANADA BY THOMAS ALLEN, LTD., TORONTO

ACKNOWLEDGMENTS

THE publication of this book is possible because of the generosity of Miss Harriet Shaw Weaver and the Estate of James Joyce, who permitted microfilm of the British Museum MSS to be made, and the Society of Authors, which authorized the printing of the texts. Acknowledgment is also made to The Viking Press, Inc., and to Faber and Faber, publishers of *Finnegans Wake*.

The Yale University Library has allowed me to see and comment on the copy for the Gaige galleys.

The Lockwood Memorial Library of the University of Buffalo has made much of its Joyce collection available to me.

The staffs of the libraries of the University of Minnesota, Kansas State University, and the University of Kansas have been helpful at many stages of my work.

The encouragement and interest of John Hinsdale Thompson, Walt Litz, Mrs. Adaline Glasheen, M. J. C. Hodgart, John Clark, David Hayman, Clive Hart, and my wife have been invaluable. The aid of all these people has been freely given, and I will not burden them with the usual recital of particulars. But the patience of my wife has been the patience of Mrs. Joyce herself.

A research grant from Kansas State University made possible the purchase of the microfilm from which this edition has been made.

FRED H. HIGGINSON

Manhattan, Kansas
June 16, 1959

TABLE OF CONTENTS

INTRODUCTION	3
EDITORIAL NOTE	16
TEXT A	23
TEXT B	28
TEXT C	36
TEXT D	47
TEXT E	60
TEXT F	78
TEXTUAL APPENDIX	99
NOTES	102
BIBLIOGRAPHICAL NOTE	111

INTRODUCTION AND EDITORIAL NOTE

INTRODUCTION

IN the fall of 1923 James Joyce had a large red-backed notebook in which he was composing early drafts of Book I of *Finnegans Wake*. We cannot be sure, of course, that this notebook contains actual first drafts of any of the chapters of Book I; but, lacking such drafts, we may begin with the notebook, which is now part of the immense collection of Joyce MSS given to the British Museum by Miss Harriet Weaver. In it is probably the first record still extant of "Anna Livia Plurabelle":

O, tell me now about Anna Livia. I want to hear all about Anna Livia. Well you know Anna Livia. Yes of course I know Anna Livia. Tell me now. Tell me now.

That is all. This germ of the introductory paragraph of ALP occurs at the end of a draft of the preceding chapter (B. M. Add. MS 47471B.68a), and not until six pages later in the notebook does Joyce settle down to producing an expanded version (reproduced later as Text A); but even that draft is incomplete; that is to say, it does not include all the material of the chapter, let alone in its final form; but it is a viable sketch, gravid with possibilities Joyce knew how to nurture into life. Even the paragraphs in the early draft which are appreciably closer than others to their final versions sound like the inefficient memorial reconstructions of a Bad Quarto. The draft represents, only too obviously, what Joyce said is the material of the chapter: the conversation of two washerwomen. The *Wake* that readers know is the product of an almost unrelenting will and a Breughelesque prodigality of detail, draft after draft, producing Art from Nature. One publishable overlay was applied to the bleak original ground of Text A in sixteen hundred hours, the time Joyce

ANNA LIVIA PLURABELLE

claimed to have spent on this chapter between its inception and the *transition* version, some four years later and still far from final. If he had worked on the whole book at the same rate, he would have been working thirty-two hours a day for the seventeen years it took him to complete it. But this was a favorite chapter; on the eve of his fifty-fifth birthday, he wrote: "Either the end of Part I [ALP] is something or I am an imbecile in my judgment of language."

His judgment was quite sound. ALP is undoubtedly the best-known and most widely read section of the *Wake*, even though, as Hugh Kenner has pointed out, it is not "representative of the entire book." But for many people it is, indeed, the only section. For these readers, unfortunately, Joyce's final work must stand or fall on the tour de force of riparian geography which is its most famous device. Significantly, that is a comparatively late device. River-names such as any-one might think of (Moldau, Ganges, Dnieper, Vistula) begin to appear only in the second typescript, and that is a fifth version of the chapter. The device may well have occurred to Joyce much earlier; but he did not begin to exploit it until he was about to publish. It is a mere device. The texts which follow offer much richer material. One sentence reads, for example, in its first draft: "My sight is getting thick now with shadows about me." In the fair copy, the sentence has become: "My sight is getting thicker on me with the shadows in this place." Still close to the literal comment of the laundress, but beginning to take on the rhythms which those who have heard the Joyce recording of this passage will recognize. The final version appears as early as the second typescript; how sweetly flows the liquefaction of the prose: "My sights are swimming thicker on me by the shadows to this place." What we have watched is not the *fait accompli*, but the *oeuvre en progrès*.

Certain of Joyce's revisions have been studied before, and it is agreed that they produce verbal refinement and complication, though these qualities are evaluated in polar ways; they are the bane of the book on the one hand or its beauty on the other, depending on whether one thinks the revisions obsessive or essential. The materials for decision are presented later in a more detailed form than has been available before, and these materials can show what makes the

INTRODUCTION

Wake more and more "that thing which it is and no other thing," to use Stephen Dedalus' words. The value of a work of art for Stephen — and for Joyce, too, if his practice in the *Wake* is any indication — lies in its being a "made" thing, of more value as it is more of an artifact. Joyce's creativity appears to move between the extremes of the facti-form in *Dubliners* to that of the arti-form in *Finnegans Wake*.

Adverse criticism of the *Wake*, whether sympathetic or unsympathetic, is largely based on the misconception that it is a novel. Thus to ally the book for life with *Tom Jones, Persuasion,* and *Studs Lonigan* is a marriage of convenience at best, and probably a morganatic one to boot. For, as Forster says, "Oh, dear me, yes, the novel tells a story." And in the *Wake* there is a constant movement away from the story in total effect. This is in fact the motion of Joyce's work as a whole: "The Dead" has more story than *Ulysses* — or at any rate, more plot, in Forster's sense — and quite possibly more than *Ulysses* and *Finnegans Wake* put together. With no story, no novel: rather a work of the fictive imagination. The *Wake* is that; and it is unique, the sole member of its class.

The movement away from story in the making of ALP will be shown by tracing a single paragraph from beginning to finished state: the one in which Anna Livia is bathing and dressing. The paragraph has some verbal parallels with Etain's bath in *The Wooing of Etain* and *The Destruction of Da Derga's Hostel*, descriptions which are themselves almost identical. And there are similar passages in Burton's translation of *The Thousand and One Nights, Iliad* XIV (the suggestion of M. J. C. Hodgart), Swinburne's "Laus Veneris," and doubtless a great many other sources. The first version of this passage reads as follows, with brackets marking insertions:

She [first] let her hair loose and down to her heels it flowed and then [mothernaked] she washed herself from crown to sole with bogwater and mudsoap [and greased her keel with butterscotch and painted beautyspots on all her skin] and then she wove a garland for her hair and pleated it and plaited it of meadowgrass and riverflags and bulrushes and waterweeds and leaves of weeping willow and then she made her bracelets and her anklets and her necklet [and her armlets amulet] of cobblestones and pebbles and rich gems and rare gems [and rhinestones and watermarbles]. And then she sent her

ANNA LIVIA PLURABELLE

[boudoir] maid to Humphrey with a request that she might leave him for a moment [and said she wouldn't be any length] and then with her bag upon her shoulder, [Anna Livia oysterface], out at last she came.

The insertions are themselves interesting. (It must be said that all of them did not occur at anything like the same time, as the reproduction of Add. MS 47471B. 75b–76a and 87b–88a (p. 8) shows; and in the later MSS, there often occur marks from several pens or pencils on the same text. But, for convenience, here and throughout, I treat all alterations in the same MS as if they were products of a single revision.) "Mothernaked" reinforces the maternal imagery associated with Anna Livia. An inclination to make jingles, and the appropriateness of them to trickling rivers, adds "armlets amulet" to the list of *-let* words. "Boudoir" may be intended even this early to add French *bou*, "mud" (the word is certainly there later). "She wouldn't be any length" reminds us that a straight line from the head of the Liffey to its mouth is a good deal less than its length. "Oysterface" is possibly intended to remind us of Tenniel's oysters illustrating "The Walrus and the Carpenter," for Carroll and his works appear somehow on almost every page of FW.

Before he made a fair copy of this paragraph at a later place in the same notebook, Joyce had made other changes. Among these is the change of "loose" to "fall": the latter is a water-word, the first is not. "Heels" is changed to "feet" for the same reason. Anna's bag becomes a "mealiebag": "meal" plus "melee" (probably in both the literal sense, "mixed," and the derived sense, "confused") plus "mail" (since, as we learn later, she has borrowed the bag from her postman son, Shaun). "Skin" becomes "little mary," which is the stomach. "Keel," in the same sentence, means "buttocks." The rest of the sentence is obscure, but it may contain a reference to a song. Tom Moore's "Rich and Rare Were the Gems She Wore" is already alluded to in the earlier version. A few more words are added or changed, and the paragraph now reads as follows:

First she let her hair fall and down it flowed to her feet and then mothernaked she washed herself with bogwater and mudsoap from her crown to her sole. Then she greased the groove of her keel with

INTRODUCTION

butterscotch and multiplied brown islands all over her little mary. Then she wove a garland for her hair. She pleated it. She plaited it. Of meadowgrass and riverflags, of bulrushes and waterweeds, of leaves of weeping willow. Then she made her bracelets and her anklets and her armlets and an amulet for necklet of cobbles and pebbles and rich gems and rare ones, of rhinestones and watershellmarbles. That done she sent her boudoir maid to Humphrey with a request that she might leave him for a moment and said she wouldn't be any length away. Then with her mealiebag slung over her shoulder, Anna Livia, oysterface, out at last she came.

Revisions between this version and the first typescript repeat and reinforce the imagery already operating; in addition, changes are made which contribute rhetorically: a further breaking-up of sentences, alteration of simple time-indicators, increase of alliteration. The "rhinestones" become "Irish," making possible the later pun on "runestones." "Watershellmarbles" becomes "shellmarble bangles." "With leafmould" is added to the sentence about the keel, reminding us of the same clutching fingers of leaf that Eliot has used; *The Waste Land* appeared in 1922, a little more than a year before these revisions, and Joyce was familiar with the poem. The "brown moles" are changed to "a thousand isles and islets dun"; the Thousand Islands, after all, are the place the dressing comes from; they are in the St. Lawrence River; and St. Lawrence is the patron saint of Dublin. "Dun" adds a river in India and possibly also the Irish word meaning a fortified hill (such as Howth). The "amulet" is made "jetty," reinforcing the dock-bridge imagery of the chapter. The text now reads:

First she let her hair fall and down it flowed to her feet. Then, mothernaked, she washed herself with bogwater and mudsoap from her crown to her sole. Next she greased the groove of her keel with butterscotch and with leafmould she multiplied a thousand isles and islets dun all over her little mary. And after that she wove a garland for her hair. She pleated it. She plaited it. Of meadowgrass and riverflags, the bulrush and waterweed, and of fallen leaves of weeping willow. Then she made her bracelets and her anklets and her armlets and a jetty amulet for necklace of clicking cobbles and pattering pebbles and rumbledown rubble, rich gems and rare, of Irish rhinestones and shellmarble bangles. That done, she sent her boudoir maid to Humphrey with a request she might leave him for a moment and said she wouldn't be any length away. Then, then, with her

ANNA LIVIA PLURABELLE

mealiebag slung over her shoulder, Anna Livia, oysterface, out at last she came.

Further changes were made between this version and the next. "Upper and lower" is added after "mudsoap," calling attention to the nature of rivers and baths. "Humphrey," the hero, becomes "His Affluence," from the Latin root meaning "flow"; the word emphasizes that even the hero is subordinate here to Anna and her characteristics. And just after this, the phrase "with respects from his missus, seepy and sewery" adds the rivers Mississippi and Missouri.

Before it was first published, Joyce again revised the chapter. Even though there are fewer changes at this point for this paragraph than for other portions of the chapter, there are still quite enough to be noticeable. The famous effects begin to appear in quantity. Joyce changes "flowed" to "flussed," adding German *Fluss*, "river." He adds "its teviots winding coils"; "teviots" is "devious" plus the river Teviot. He adds "turfentine" and "serpenthyme" ("serpentine" plus the twisting imagery plus a thyme-fixation; the Serpentine in Phoenix Park is the site of the barrow with the crucial letter uncovered by the hen). "Multiplied" is changed to "ushered round," adding Usher's Quay, Dublin, and possibly also the river Usch. "A thousand isles" is changed to "prunella isles," adding the river Prunelli and possibly a complicated conflation arising from French *prunelle*, "pupil of the eye" and the island off Howth Head called Ireland's Eye. "Leaves" becomes "griefs," a change of a word to one phonetically similar, but delicately more evocative. "Rich gems and rare" becomes "richmond and rare," adding another river and Richmond Bridge, Dublin. With the phrase "a dawk of smut to her airy ey" is added a group of rivers (Daugava, Smutua, Aire, and Ey); further, Old Norse *ey* means "island"; and the "dawk-dock" pun looks forward to the mailbag and the mud. "Boudoir" becomes "boudeloire," confirming the *bou* pun, adding the river Loire and Baudelaire, whose poem "Correspondances" Joyce knew and which has relevance to the invoking of rivers Joyce is doing. "Respects" becomes "respecks"; obviously, there is an imitation of speech; but the hen pecks at the letter, and the salmon and trout mentioned throughout the chapter are speckled, and there is a "dawk of smut" in the context. "Moment" becomes

Typical pages from the large red-backed notebook

INTRODUCTION

"minnikin," which is possibly "minute" plus "mannikin," but which is also immediately communicative: a little bit. The paragraph now reads, in its first published version:

First she let her hair fall and down it flussed to her feet its teviots winding coils. Then, mothernaked, she washed herself with bogwater and mudsoap, upper and lower from crown to sole. Next she greased the groove of her keel with antifouling butterscotch and turfentine and serpenthyme and with leafmould she ushered round prunella isles and islets dun all over her little mary. And after that she wove a garland for her hair. She pleated it. She plaited it. Of meadowgrass and riverflags, the bulrush and waterweed, and of fallen griefs of weeping willow. Then she made her bracelets and her anklets and her armlets and a jetty amulet for necklace of clicking cobbles and pattering pebbles and rumbledown rubble, richmond and rare or [sic] Irish rhinestones and shellmarble bangles. That done, a dawk of smut to her airy ey and she sent her boudeloire maid to His Affluence, with respecks from his missus, seepy and sewery, and a request might she leave him for a minnikin. She said she wouldn't be half her length away. Then, then, with her mealiebag slung over her shoulder, Anna Livia, oysterface, out at last she came.

After this version, Joyce had a chance to work over several sets of proof for the next publication. By this time the revisions are becoming more and more matters of detail; but more and more we have to go out of the immediate context to make sense of an alteration; more and more of them add to the replication which is characteristic of the book as a whole. "Washed" becomes "sampood," suggesting "shampooed" and the river Sampna. "Bogwater" gives way to "galawater" (a river), a word appropriate to the context, since Anna Livia eventually goes to a party. After "keel" comes "warthes and wears and mole and itcher": "warthes" is "warts" plus a river; "wears" is "weirs" plus a river; "mole" is a river, with possibly a hint of Latin *moles*, "sea-wall" (and note the return to an idea of the first draft); "itcher" suggests the river Itchen. The list of cosmetics is extended: "the lellipos cream to her lippeleens and the pick of the paintbox for her pommettes, from strawbirry reds to extray violates." "Lellipos" jingles with "lippeleens" and is possibly formed from Greek *leloipa*, "forsaken" and *lipos*, "fat" and may mean something like "vanishing cream" or "leftovers." There are also overtones of the *Journal to*

ANNA LIVIA PLURABELLE

Stella. "Lippeleens" adds the rivers Lippe and Ipel and ends with a common Irish diminutive. "Pommettes" is French for "cheekbones," conflated with "pomade." "Strawbirry reds" yields the Strawberry Beds, a Liffey-side sight, and Birr, a town called "Umbilicus Hiberniae" by Sir William Petty (mentioned later in the chapter). The spectrum runs to ultraviolet: "violates" reinforces the atmosphere of peril which surrounds Anna (elsewhere in the chapter, she is "on the vierge violetian"). The spectrum itself recalls the seven rainbow girls who accompany her. The one maid becomes two, and they are given names, "Ciliegia Grande and Kirschie Real," the first names reflecting the Italian and German words for "cherry" and the surnames being both honorifics and the names of rivers. A sentence of explanation for Anna's absence is added: "A call to pay and light a taper, in Brie-on-Arrosa, back in a sprizzling." For "sprizzling," Joyce originally wrote "sprinkling," but later chose the Italian root *sprizz-*, possibly because it means both "spurt" and "speckled." "Brie-on-Arrosa" bears a resemblance to phrases elsewhere in FW (the name O'Brien Rossa emerges from them); here the phrase ought to be a reference to some Dublin church. But there is a river Arros; Irish *bri* means "hill"; hence it is possible to read "the hill by the river," another reference to Howth. Another sentence is added: "The cock [a boat] striking mine [a river], the stalls [the river Talla] bridely [the river Bride] sign [the river Sig], there's Zambosy [the river Zambezi] waiting for Me!" The undertone of this heavily aqueous passage is probably a popular song: "The clock striking nine, the stars brightly shine, there's somebody waiting for me." Finally, before the "mealiebag" sentence, Joyce adds "as soon as the lump his back was turned," and this clause carries suggestions of German *Lumpenpack*, which would freely translate "mealiebag" and which suggests the hunchback Humphrey sometimes has. The paragraph now reads:

First she let her hair fall and down it flussed to her feet its teviots winding coils. Then, mothernaked, she sampood herself with galawater and mudsoap, upper and lower from crown to sole. Next she greased the groove of her keel, warthes and wears and mole and itcher, with antifouling butterscotch and turfentine and serpen-

INTRODUCTION

thyme and with leafmould she ushered round prunella isles and islets dun all over her little mary. And after that she wove a garland for her hair. She pleated it. She plaited it. Of meadowgrass and riverflags, the bulrush and waterweed, and of fallen griefs of weeping willow. Then she made her bracelets and her anklets and her armlets and a jetty amulet for necklace of clicking cobbles and pattering pebbles and rumbledown rubble, richmond and rare, of Irish rhinestones and shellmarble bangles. That done, a dawk of smut to her airy ey and the lellipos cream to her lippeleens and the pick of the paintbox for her pommettes, from strawbirry reds to extray violates, and she sent her boudeloire maids to His Affluence — Ciliegia Grande and Kirschie Real [—] with respecks from his missus, seepy and sewery, and a request she might leave him for a minnikin. A call to pay and light a taper, in Brie-on-Arrosa, back in a sprizzling. The cock striking mine, the stalls bridely sign, there's Zambosy waiting for me. She said she wouldn't be half her length away. Then, then, as soon as the lump his back was turned, with her mealiebag slung over her shoulder, Anna Livia, oysterface, out of her basin came.

There is not now very much to do to bring this paragraph to its final state. These final revisions are important, but if we recall that they appear to take Joyce ten years, as compared with the five taken to reach the version just quoted, they seem inordinately time-consuming. It is true that Joyce's eyes were giving him more and more trouble and that he had become tired of the book, at one time thinking of turning it over to James Stephens to finish; but, most important, many other chapters of the book were in by no means so finished a state as ALP, and Joyce worked at the revisions of these. The final ten per cent or so of the revision of ALP, therefore, corresponds to as much as fifty per cent or more in other sections.

To finish this paragraph, Joyce changes "fall" to "fal," which is both a river and an Irish word meaning "fold" (like the twisting Liffey) and "circle" (like the cyclic process of Vico). "Butterscotch" becomes "butterscatch," adding the river Tersa and emphasizing a "buttery catch" pun. "Mudsoap" becomes "fraguant pistania mud"; "fraguant" is "fragrant" and the river Fragua, plus Spanish *agua*, "water" and perhaps Latin *fragum*, "strawberry," linking with "strawbirry." "Pistania" may be "pistacia" (one of the *turpentine* trees) plus the river Istaneh; and it may contain French

11

ANNA LIVIA PLURABELLE

piste, "scent": Anna can be thought of as leaving a kind of trail. "Greased" is changed to "greesed," adding the river Reese. "Upper" becomes "wupper" (a river); "lower" becomes "lauar," adding the river Laua. "Turfentine" becomes "turfentide," adding "tide" to "thyme." "Islets" becomes "eslats," adding the river Esla. "Quincecunct" is added to describe the quincunctial pattern of the leafmould and perhaps to mean "fifteen times" (Spanish *quince,* "fifteen" plus Latin *cunctus,* "all together"); and there is an obscene overtone. "All over" is run together, adding the river Allow. One whole sentence of description is added: "Peeld gold of waxwork her jellybelly and her grains of incense anguille bronze." There are rivers (Jellei and Belly), and possibly there is a reference to Enobarbus' barge speech, and certainly French *anguille,* "eel" adds to the twisting imagery, but the complete sense and purpose of the sentence is obscure to me. "Rare" is changed to "rehr," a river. "Rhinestones" becomes "rhunerhinestones," making the allusion to "runestone" unmistakable. Anna is given a pseudonym, "Annushka Lutetiavitch Pufflovah," which probably means something like "Little Anne, the Parisienne (from Latin *Lutetia,* "Paris"), Pavlova-Luvah-pufflover." Luvah is one of Blake's Four Zoas. The puff may merely be the one Anna is using at the moment; but the entire word may make Anna someone who likes a pipesmoker, which one of her sons is. "Sent" becomes "sendred," adding the river Endre. "The two chirsines" reinforces "Ciliegia" and "Kirschie" and in addition suggests "chorine" and the river Chirin. "Leave" becomes "passe of," adding French *passer,* "to go," a typical bilingual reinforcement, and also perhaps Danish *passe,* "wait on, serve," and "pass him off." "Slung" becomes "slang," adding the river Langa and Irish English "a narrow strip of land along a stream, not suitable for cultivation, but grazed." "Shoulder" becomes "shulder," adding another bilingual reinforcement, German *Schulter.* "Out" is changed to "forth," adding a river. Finally, "basin" becomes "bassein," adding a river and Italian *bassa,* "shallows." At last we have the version of FW (206.29 ff.).

The original draft (of less complexity, surely, than *Ulysses*) has been rendered by the revisions semantically dense and sometimes syntactically difficult. The immediate impression of facetation which

INTRODUCTION

the text is sure to make can be seen by an examination of the revisions to be a way of concentrating, rather than of diffusing, the light; and that the text does not often suggest more than it does witnesses the complete security with which Joyce went about his lapidary process. In revising, he employs a mosaic technique: the text is bits put together; then, so to speak, he spreads out the pieces, preserving the original outline of the picture, and puts in more pieces; then he squeezes the frame back to its former size, or thereabouts. From a reader's point of view, the farther he is away from the mosaic the more it looks like "what it is"; the closer he is, the more it looks like a collection of pieces of colored rock stuck together with grout, the more like a magnified Seurat. The chief characteristic of the language of the book results, then, from frame-squeezing: the morphemes have no place to go but together.

All of the tedious aspects of revision are directed, as are also the more inspired, toward strengthening the structure of the book. The very language of FW is a structural device in that word combinations can indicate or intensify relationships between materials being used. Every river-name in ALP is supposed to remind us that the chapter is about Anna, who is the Liffey, which represents all most-beautiful rivers. The *Wake* version probably contains something like eight hundred river-names; yet, in the first draft, none. Revision does it all. Searching for rivers to fit the text was done not only by Joyce, but, rumor has it, also by colleagues, amanuenses, a grandchild, and houseguests: anyone who would feed the obsession. And such perseverance and perfectionism are typical of the composition of the book as a whole.

As one might expect, ALP is also full of words meaning "river," "shore," "riverbank," "sea," "harbor," "quay," "brook," "well," "dam," "boat," "wash," "herring-trout-salmon," "fountain," "water," etc., words having to do with the river itself, its geographical features, the life within it and around it, extending finally to quite incidentally watery objects like the "codfisck ee" of the hero. Some of the words in this class are of necessity in the first published text, but a good many more (both in English and in other languages) were added before the second publication. Obviously, Joyce was, at least

13

ANNA LIVIA PLURABELLE

at first, more interested in this water cluster than he was in the better-known device of the actual river-names. Since neither device is exhaustible, within the limits Joyce set himself, it is an indication of his interests that he had enough of both sorts of material left over to furnish a reprise of much the same type in the final chapter of FW.

Of all things watery, let alone rivers, Joyce's favorite is the Liffey, which flows through Dublin after a seventy-mile run from its head some thirteen miles away as the "croaker" flies, a meandering course which is indicated all through the chapter by means of the "twist" imagery. Localities on or near the river also furnish material: Hazelhatch, Lucan, the Strawberry Beds, Kippure, Sally Gap, Spa, Clane, the Golden Falls, Pollaphuca, Carrigacurra, to refer only to large-scale maps. When the river reaches Dublin, its course can be followed from Phoenix Park at one end of the city to the Pigeonhouse and the Irish Sea at the other, under the Dublin bridges and quays. Of Dublin, there are not only the guidebook items, like Capel Street, but also the esoteric, like Standfast Dick, a rock outcrop in the Liffey. As the Irish critics are fond of pointing out (especially to Americans), no one but a Dubliner, with Joyce the Dublinest of all, could hope to garner nearly all the references he sows. But what is probably most significant about these references anyway is that well over half the ones which impinge on one non-Dubliner are planted in the text by the time of its first publication, which means that Joyce thought them more important structurally than either the water-words or the river-names. However, no matter what device we choose, Joyce's structural use of language is conspicuous and pervasive.

Such a use of language is intimately related to what is enjoyable about FW, which is essentially the pleasure of watching the mind at work, as it is in Euclid, Mendelejeff, or Beethoven's notebooks, FW being a Work in Progress, being no more totally complete than geometry, or the atomic table, or a late quartet. What makes FW a great book is that there is in it as much of these pleasurable workings of one man's mind — the whole of it, shoddy and magnificent both — as has ever been put between covers. Joyce's problem with it, as it had been with *Ulysses*, was how to hold together diverse and cha-

INTRODUCTION

otic materials, those of FW being the infinitely more complex. Therefore, if the book is to be in any sense Art, its structure has to take precedence over its materials, the troublesomeness of which arises largely from their intractable triviality. The narrative base on which Joyce builds is in itself flimsy and largely uninteresting, as are parallel lines and molecules and thematic materials. What holds our attention is the superstructure rather than the foundation; the superstructure — the book's synthetic becoming — is what the pains of revision are lavished on. The problem of holding a book together had been engaging Joyce; he invented a language which in itself would be a cohesive force in the book he was writing, and this solution works. There can be little doubt that FW is more unified than *Ulysses*: it is less chapter-y; it is less episodic; and though the manner is capable of many moods, the language is centripetal. The rationale of the language is that FW is declared to be a dream, an ALP-*traum* perhaps, but still the wit and the intensity of the language may thus be justified. Beginning with "word in pregross," we end with "The Log of Anny to the Base All." Nothing happens in the book by chance; *alp*, by convenient natural luck, is the Brythonic word meaning "color," and hence the seven Rainbow Girls may be introduced into the story. The wordy tissue of FW is formed of just such correspondences yoked by patient cunning together.

EDITORIAL NOTE

THE purpose of this book is to show the development of the text of ALP, accounting for every emendation which brought the text from its earliest extant state to that in FW. Because of the way in which Joyce revised ALP, seldom omitting anything and mainly adding to or conflating the text in front of him, rather than recasting the text in a wholesale fashion, it became clear early in the process of editing that a system of brackets could be adopted which, when combined with the necessary notes, would permit the concurrent publication of two or more texts with their emendations. It is therefore possible for a scholar to recover from the texts given in this book Joyce's texts (or, in a few instances, what my best judgment tells me Joyce's intended text was) in all of the extant versions of this chapter, punctuation excepted. This quite extensive material has been condensed into six texts and an appendix, in the following manner:

Text A. A transcript of the partial first draft, dating probably from autumn, 1923. MS 47471B.73–78.

Text B. A transcript of the second draft, dating also probably from autumn, 1923. MS 47471B.79–90.

Text C. This text is a composite of a fair copy and a typescript made from the fair copy. Both versions were sent to Miss Weaver March 8, 1924. The fair copy (MS 47474.107–118) is emended enough on five pages (MS 47474.119–123, numbered 5, 6, 10–12) that Joyce recopied them for the typist. Furthermore, since there are various emendations incorporated in the typescript (MS 47474.125–140) which appear nowhere in Joyce's hand, and since there are cer-

EDITORIAL NOTE

tain sheets which contain verso corrections incorporated into the following recto typescript, it would appear that what is called the "first" typescript is not that throughout, but is at least in part a second. Pages 1, 1', 5, 5', and 9–11 probably are retyped versions, while 2–4, 6–8, and [12] are simply copies of the fair copy.

Texts A, B, and C reproduce exactly all spelling and punctuation, since the first two represent texts entirely in Joyce's hand and the third one mainly so, though there are a few additions of which no holograph record appears to exist. With Text D this convention is modified, and with Texts E and F abandoned, since it seemed merely lugubrious to reproduce errata which were the fault of a typist, amanuensis, or typesetter, which in most instances Joyce never allowed to be published, and which lack even orthographic interest. Account is of course taken in the notes of errors which affect the published text or which are of interest otherwise. The general policy is this: Joyce's holograph is authoritative and, lacking that, a published text. But since Joyce's punctuation is often defective, I have made it conform, without annotation (in Texts D, E, and F), to the latest text with which I am dealing in a given composite and have extended this rule to cover hyphenization, capitalization, and accent marks. Joyce made a few emendations which do not appear in any published text; my own feeling here is that if he had felt they mattered a great deal, he would have seen that they became part of his text. Since he did not, I take account of them only in the notes.

Text Ḋ. This text is a composite of a second typescript (incomplete, MS 47474.160–166), a third typescript (three sets, MS 47474.142–159, 168–184, 186–202), and a partial set of galleys for the *Calendar* (MS 47474.204–206), for which at least part of ALP was set up, but in which it never appeared. The galleys date from July, 1925 (see the letter to Miss Sylvia Beach, July 25, in *Letters*), the typescripts necessarily preceding. Joyce revised both the first and second sets of the third typescript, though not identically, and these emendations have been combined on the third set in a hand identified by Miss Weaver as that of Miss Beach. The *Calendar* galleys were set from this third set of the typescript.

Text E. This text is a composite of the text of ALP published in *Le*

ANNA LIVIA PLURABELLE

Navire d'Argent (October, 1925), 61–74; of galleys for *transition* (MS 47474.209–225); of the text of ALP published in *transition 8* (November, 1927), 17–35; and of three paged sets of *transition*. The printed text of the first of these sets (MS 47474.227–246) antedates that of the published version and contains many errors, none of which is corrected, since Joyce used this set only for the indication of additions. The second (MS 47474.248–257) is corrected in the hand of an amanuensis and contains the additions on the first set plus some others; the printed text is identical with that published in *transition*. The third set is the copy for the galleys of the Gaige edition of ALP; this set is now in the Yale University Library. It is dated February 2, 1928, Joyce's forty-sixth birthday, and contains a few corrections not on the second paged set, which was probably the copy Joyce kept for his own reference. The first paged set may be the one Joyce is talking about in his letter of October 29, 1927, to Miss Weaver, and the second that described in the letter of November 9, also to Miss Weaver, though the figures given for changes in both letters are too low for the number actually present in the MSS.

Text F. This text is a composite of the Gaige galleys (MS 47474.-259–271), further revisions of the Gaige galleys, the Gaige ALP, and the Faber ALP. The Gaige galleys are dated February 10–13, 1928, at the Princeton University Press; they are corrected in Joyce's hand, but not sufficiently to produce the text of the Gaige ALP as published. A further set of revisions must therefore be postulated; this revised copy is at present unlocated. The Gaige (New York, 1928) and Faber and Faber (London, 1930) texts of ALP differ only slightly. There seems to be a slight discrepancy between the date on the copy for the galleys (Paris, 2/2/28) and that on the galleys themselves (Princeton, 2/10/28); this I cannot explain.

Textual Appendix. The Faber and Faber ALP was used by Joyce as the copy for the galleys of FW. The British Museum collection contains two sets of these corrected texts of ALP (MS 47475.75–90, 164–179). There are, in addition, a few revisions on the galleys themselves (MS 47476A.118–132, 261–275; MS 47476B.411–425). The textual appendix lists these late changes; for a very few there appears to be no extant authority.

EDITORIAL NOTE

A bracket in the texts which follow (except A and part of B) indicates that a change has taken place between this text and the ones preceding. The more brackets, the later the change. Unless there is a note, a set of brackets means that, up to the text represented by the bracketing, there has been no change; if there has been a previous change, a note explains it. Footnotes explain usage of brackets in particular texts.

TEXTS

TEXT A

O TELL me all now about Anna Livia. I want to know all about Anna Livia. Well, you know Anna Livia? Yes, of course, I know Anna. Tell me all. Tell me now. You'll die when you hear. Well, you see, when the old chap did what you know. Yes, I know, go on. Or whatever it was [they try to make out] he [tried to do] [1] in the [2] [Phoenix] park. He's an awful old rep. What was it he did at all? It was [put] in the papers what he did. [Time will tell. I know it will] O, the old rep! What age is he at all at all? [Or where was he born or how was he found? Don't you know he's [3] a bairn of the sea, Waterhouse the waterbaby? O, I know, so he was. HCE has blue in his ee.] Sure, she's nearly as bad herself. Who? Anna Livia? Yes, Anna Livia. Do you know that she was calling girls into him? She was? Ah, go to God! O, tell me all I want to hear. Letting on she didn't care. Didn't you see her at [her windeye] [4] pretending to play [a fiddle she has without a bottom]? [5] Sure she can't play the [fiddle]. [6] Of course she can't, [bottom or not], it was all a blind. Well, I never heard the like of that. Tell me more. Tell me all. Well, the old chap was a [7] glum as [could be], [8] sitting moping all by himself [on his benk his hair combed over his eyes dreeing his weird keeking on loft staring up at the sternes] [9] and there was Anna Livia running about as if she was [a girl] ten in a short [summer] skirt and painted cheeks [10] [and an odd time she meddering [11] him up blooms [12] of fisk and eyes to plaise him and as quick as she'd run with [13] them up on her [14] tray the old chap'd cast them from him if he didn't peg the tea at her] trying to whistle the Rakes of Mallow and not a [mag] [15] out of him no more than the wall. Is that a fact? That's a fact.

NOTE: This text is a transcript of the first extant draft, with emendations indicated by brackets.

ANNA LIVIA PLURABELLE

And do you know what she started singing then [like a water gluck]? You'll never guess. Tell me. Tell me. I loved you better than you knew [and calling [16] to him down the feedchute: Hello ducky, please don't die and letting on to rave about the old songs [17] from over the holm High hellsker saw ladies [18] hen smoke a pigger, the powder pouring off her nose] Ah, go to God, is it Anna Livia? As God is my judge. And then she'd [trot down] [19] and stand in the door and every servant girl that [went the road] [20] she'd make [her] a sign to step inside [by the sallyport]. You don't say, [the sallyport]! I [did]! [21] I do! Calling them all [22] [and legging [23] a jig or two to show them how to shake their benders and how to show what's out of sight and all the way of a maid with a man, cuddle and squiggle and bill and coo, and making a kind of a cackling noise like half a crown [24] and holding up a silver shiner].[25] Well, of all the things ever I heard! [To any girl at all of no matter what sex of playful ways] A half a crown [26] [a go] to sit and [have] [27] fun in Humpy's lap!

[And what about the rhyme she made up. O that! Tell me that. I'm dying down off my feet until I hear. How does it go? Well, listen now.

[By earth and heaven but I want a brandnew backside badly, bedad and I do, and a plumper [28] at that

[For the putty affair [29] I have is worn out, so it is, sitting down [30] yawning and waiting for my [31] old Dane the dodderer,[32] my frugal key of the larder [33] my [34] muchaltered camel's hump, my jointspoiler, my maymoon's honey my fool to the last [35] Decemberer, to wake up out of his doze [36] and shout [37] me down like he used to.

[Is there any [38] lord of the manor [39] at all'd give me a pound or two [40] I wonder for washing his socks [41] for him now that we're run out of meat and milk? [42]

[Only for my bed is as [43] warm as it smells it's up I'd leap [44] and off with me to the Bull of Clontarf to get the kind air of Dublin [45] bay and the race of the seawind up my hole]

O go on and tell me more. Tell me every [little bit.] [46] I want to know every single thing. Well, now comes the childer's part. How many childer has she at all? [I can't rightly tell you that.] God only knows. I hear she has 111. [She can't remember half their names.]

24

TEXT A

A hundred and how? They did well to [christen] [47] her Plurabelle. O, my! Such a flock! She must have been a gadabout in her day, so she must. So she was, you bet. Tell me, tell me, [how did she come through all her fellows], who was the 1st [that ever burst? That's a thing I always wish to know.] She says herself she [hardly] [48] knew who he was or what he did or where [49] he crossed her. She was a young thin pale slip of a thing then and he was a heavy lurching Curraghman [as strong as the oaks there used to be that time down in killing Kildare] that first fell across her. You're wrong there. You're all wrong. It was ages [50] before [that] in the county Wicklow the garden of Erin before she ever dreamt [51] she'd end in [the barleyfields and her pennylands [52] of] Humphreystown and lie [53] with a landleaper, well on the wane. Was it, was it? [Are [54] you sure?] Where in Wicklow? Tell me where, the very first time. [I will if you listen You know the glen] [55] there near Luggelaw [Well, once there dwelt] one day in [June [56] in smiling mood] and so young and shy and so limber she looked he [plunged both of his] his [blessed] [57] hands [up to his wrists] in her flowing hair, that was rich red like this brown bog and he couldn't help [it], thirst was too hot for him, he cooled his lips [kiss after kiss] [58] at Anna Livia's freckled cheek. [O wasn't he the bold priest! O wasn't she the naughty Livia? Naughtynaughty is her name. Two lads in their breeches went through her before that, Barefoot [59] Byrne and Billy Wade, before she had a hint of hair there to hide, and ere that again she was licked by a hound when doing her pee, sweet and simple, on the side of a hill in shearingtime [60] but first of all [61] and worst of all she ran [62] through a gap when the nurse was asleep and fell before she found her stride and wriggled under a cow] [But] Why was she freckled? How long was her hair? O go on, go on, go on! I mean about what you know. I know [well] what you mean. I'm going on Where did I stop? Don't stop. Go on, go on.

Well, after it was put in the papers everywhere ever you went [and every bung [63] ever you dropped into or wherever you scoured the countryside] you found his picture upside down [or the cornerboys burning his guy] so she made a plan, the mischiefmaker, the like of it now, you never heard. What plan. Tell me quickly! What the mischief did she do? Well, she borrowed a bag, a mailbag, from

ANNA LIVIA PLURABELLE

one of her sons, Shaun the Post, and then she went and made herself up. O, [God of gigglers], I can't tell you. It's too funny. [O, but you must. You must really. I'd give my chance of going to heaven to hear it all, every word] Here, sit down, go easy, be quiet. Tell me slowly. Take your time. Breathe deeply. That's the way. Slowlier.

She [first] let her hair [fall] [64] and down to her heels it flowed and then [mothernaked] she washed herself from crown to sole with bogwater and mudsoap [and greased her keel with butterscotch and multiplied moles [65] all [66] over little mary], and then she wove a garland for her hair [67] and pleated it and plaited it of meadowgrass and riverflags and bulrushes and waterweeds and leaves of weeping willow and then she made her bracelets and her anklets and her necklet [and her armlets amulet] of cobblestones [68] and pebbles and rich gems and rare [ones] [69] and rhinestones and watermarbles. And then she sent her [boudoir] maid to Humphrey with a request that she might leave him for a moment [and said she wouldn't be any length] and then with her [mealiebag] [70] upon her shoulder, [Anna Livia oysterface], out at last she came.

Describe her! I must hear that. What had she on? What did she carry? Here she [comes].[71] What has she got? A loin of jubilee mutton.

I'll tell you now [72] but you must sit still. [Will you hold your peace listen well to what I am going to say?] The door of the [ugly] igloo opened outward and out [stepped] [73] a [fairy] woman the height of your knee. Go away! No more? The height of your knee. She wore a pair of [74] ploughman's [nailstudded] [75] boots, a sugarloaf hat [with a sunrise peak [76] and a band of gorse and] with a golden pin [through it]; owlglasses screened [77] her eyes, a pair of potato rings [buckled the loose ends of] [78] her ears: nude cuba stockings [were] salmon [spot] speckled:[79] bloodorange knickers [fancy fastened showed natural] [80] nigger bockers: her blackstriped tan joseph was teddybearlined [with a swansdown border]: a couple of gaspers stuck in [her] hayrope garters: her civvy coat was [zoned by a] [81] twobar belting She had a [tight] clothespeg astride of her nose [82] and something in her mouth as well and the tail of her snuffbrown [83] skirt trailed 50 miles behind her on the road.

TEXT A

Here the text breaks off. But suggestions for what eventually follows occur on two pages facing the text just printed. These suggestions are given below, with asterisks prefixed to those crossed out by Joyce. On B. M. Add. MS 47471B.76b:

*Bully Hayes
de Vereker
*Larry the Puckaun
Jacky Colthurst
*(jigsaw puzzle) Llewelyn Marriage
Mannix
*(acid drops) Pender's nephew

*Luckless Joe
*Pudge Craig (puffpuff)
*Wally Meagher
Boy [Kid] McCormack [84]
*Toucher Doyle
*Tommy the Soldier (a tube of cockaleekie soup)
*Buck Jones

On B. M. Add. MS 47471B.77b:

Kitty Rivers
*Gipsy Lee (tinker's tan and bucket)
*poor little Petite O'Hara (rattle and cough and rosy cheeks)
*Brown B brown betty [85]
Ann Doyle (An dáil)[86]
*Mary Selina

Isabel Murray
Evadne Bell
*Elsie Oram
Lady Betty [87]
*Kitty Coleraine
Nora Kildara
*Mary Stakelum
*Nancy Shannon

╭ ╭ TEXT B

O TELL me all now about Anna Livia! I want to [hear] all about Anna Livia. Well, you know Anna Livia? Yes, of course [we all] know Anna [Livia]. Tell me all. Tell me now. You'll die when you hear. Well, you see, when the old chap [went and] did what you know. Yes, I know, go on. [Wash away and don't be dabbling] Or whatever it was they try to make out he tried to do in the Phoenix park. He's an awful old rep. [Look at the shirt of him. Look at the dirt of it.] [1] What was it he did at all? It was put in the papers what he did. [But] time will tell. I know it will. O, the old [old] rep! What age is he at all at all? Or where was he born or how was he found? [And were him and her ever spliced?] [2] Don't you know he's a bairn of the sea, Waterhouse the waterbaby? O, I know, so he was. H.C.E has blue in his ee. Sure, she's nearly as bad [as him] [3] herself. Who, Anna Livia? [Ay], Anna Livia! Do you know she was calling girls [to go in and tickle] [4] him? She was? Go to God! O, tell me all I want to hear! Letting on she didn't care. Didn't you see her [in] her windeye pretending to play [a tune or two] a fiddle she has without a bottom? Sure, she can't play the fiddle, bottom or not. Of course, she can't. It was all a blind. Well, I never heard the like of that. Tell me more. Tell me all.

Well, old [humper] was [as] glum as [a grampus], sitting moping on his benk [hungerstriking] by himself, his hair combed over his eyes, dreeing his weird, [with his dander up holding doomsday over himself, and] keeking on loft [5] at [the face] the sternes and there [she] was, Anna Livia, [she couldn't snatch a wink of sleep], run-

NOTE: This text is a transcript of the first complete draft, with emendations indicated by brackets.

TEXT B

ning [around like] a girl [of] ten in a short summer skirt and painted cheeks. And an odd time [she'd cook] him up blooms of fisk and [meddery] eyes to plaise him [and stay his stomach] and as quick as she'd run with them up on [the] tray the old chap'd cast them from him [with a scowl], if he didn't peg the tea [in] her [face believe me she was safe enough. And then she'd try] to whistle [a tune *The Heart Bowed Down* or] *The Rakes of Mallow* [What harm if she knew how to cock her mouth?] and not a mag out of him no more than the wall. Is that a fact? That's a fact. And [cheeping] to him down the feedchute [with all kinds of fondling endings] the powder [tumbling] off her nose [Vuggybarney!⁶ Wickerymandy!] Hello, ducky! Please don't die! Do you know what she started singing then [with a voice on her] like a water gluck? You'll never guess. Tell me. Tell me. [Phoebe dearest tell, O tell me and] I loved you better than you knew. And letting on [she was daft] about the old songs from over the holm: High [hellskirt] saw ladies hen smoke a [lilyhung] ⁷ pigger. [Go away!] Is it Anna Livia. As God is my judge. And then [didn't she go and] trot down and stand in the door and every [country wench and farmerette going] the road [usedn't she] make her a sign to [slip] inside by the sallyport. You don't say the sallyport? I did. I do. Calling them [one by one] and legging a jig or two to show them how to shake their benders and [the dainty how to bring to mind the gladdest garments] out of sight and all the way of a maid with a man and making a kind of a cackling noise like [two and a penny or] half a crown and holding up a silver shiner. Well of all the [ones] ever I heard! [Lordy, lordy, Throwing all the girls in the world at him!] To any [lass] of no matter what sex of playful ways [two and a tanner a girl] a go to sit and have fun in Humpy's lap!

And what about the rhyme she made! O that! Tell me that! I'm dying down off my feet until I hear [Anna Livia's rhyme. I can see that. I can see you are.] How does it go? Listen now. [This is the rhyme Anna Livia made]

By earth and heaven but I badly want a brandnew backside, bedad and I do, and a plumper at that

For the putty affair I have is worn out, so it is, sitting, yawning and waiting for my old Dane the dodderer, [my life in death com-

ANNA LIVIA PLURABELLE

panion] my frugal key of the larder, my much altered camel's hump, my jointspoiler, my maymoon's honey, my fool to the last Decemberer, to wake up out of his [winter's] doze and shout me down like he used to.

Is there [a] lord of the manor [or a knight of the shire going] at all, I wonder, [that'd tip] me a pound or two [in cash] for washing [and darning] his [worshipful] socks for him now we're run out of [horsemeat] and milk?

Only for my [featherbed] is as [snug] as it smells it's [out] I'd [lep] and off with me to [the mouth of the Tolka or] the Bull of Clontarf to [feel] the [gay] air of [my sweet] Dublin bay and the race of the seawind up my hole!

O go on! Tell me more! Tell me every [tiny] bit! I want to [hear] every single thing. Well, now comes the childer's part. How many childer has she at all? I can't rightly tell you that God only know.[8] [They say] she [had] 111. She can't remember half [the] names [she put on them]. A hundred and how. They did [right] to christen her Plurabelle. O [laws]! [What] a flock! She must have been a gadabout in her day, so she must [more than most]. So she was, you bet. Tell me, tell me, how did she come through all her fellows, [the daredevil]? Who was the first that ever burst? [Someone it was, whoever you are. Tinker, tailor, soldier, sailor, Paul pry or polishman] That's [the] thing I always [want] to know. [Well, she can't put her hand on him for the moment] She says herself she hardly knew who he was or what he did or [when] he crossed her. She was [just] a young thin pale slip of a thing then [sauntering] and he was a heavy lurching [lieabroad] Curraghman [making hay for the sun to shine] as strong as the oaks there used to [grow] that time in killing Kildare that first fell across her. You're wrong there. You're all wrong. It was ages [long] before that in the county Wicklow, the garden of Erin, before she ever dreamt she'd end in the barleyfields and pennylands of Humphreystown and lie with a landleaper, well on the wane. Was it, was it? Are you sure? Where in Wicklow? Tell me where, the very first time! I will if you listen. You know the [hazel dell of] Luggelaw? Well,[9] there once dwelt [a local hermit named Michael Orkney [10] and] one day in [warm] June so young and shy and so limber she

TEXT B

looked, [the kind of curves you simply can't stop feeling], he plunged both of his blessed [anointed] hands up to his wrists in [the streams of] her hair that was rich red like [the] brown bog. And he couldn't help [it], thirst was too hot for him, [he had to forget the monk in the man] he cooled his lips in smiling mood kiss after kiss [on] Anna Livia's freckled cheek. O, wasn't he the bold priest! [And] wasn't she the naughty [Livvy]! Naughtynaughty is her name. Two lads in their breeches went through her before that, Barefoot Byrne and Billy Wade, [Lugnaquilla's noble pair] before she had a hint of [a] hair there to hide and ere that again she was licked by a hound [while] doing her pee, sweet and simple, on the side of [the] hill [of old Kippure] in [birdsong and] shearing time but first of all, worst of all, she [sideslipped out by] [11] a gap [in the devil's glen] when [her] nurse was [sound] asleep [in a sloot] and fell before she found her stride [and lay] and wriggled under a [fallow] cow.

[Tell me the sound [12] of the shorthorn's name [13] and tell me] why [the something] was she freckled [as well and tell me too] how long was her hair [or was it only a wig she wore? Are you in this game or are you not?] O go on, go on, go on! I mean about what you know. I know well what you mean. I'm going on. Where did I stop. Don't stop. [Continuation! You're not there yet.] Go on, go on!

Well, after it was put in the [Beggar's Journal] everywhere ever you went and every bung you ever dropped into or wherever you scoured the countryside you found his picture upside down or the cornerboys burning his guy [and Pat the Man raising a laugh reeling and rolling around the local with oddfellow's [14] triple tiara busby rotundarinking [15] round his scalp],[16] so she [said to herself she'd make] a plan [to make a shine], the mischiefmaker, the like of it now you never heard. What plan? Tell me quickly. What the mischief did she do? Well, she borrowed a bag, a mailbag from one of her sons, Shaun the Post, and then she went and made herself up. O, God of gigglers, I can't tell [how]! It's too [screaming] funny, [rabbit it all]! O but you must, you must really! [By the holy well of Mulhuddart I swear] I'd give my chance of going to heaven to hear it all, every word. Here, sit down [and do as you're told], go easy, [keep] quiet. Tell me [slow]. Take your time [now]. Breathe [deep]. That's

ANNA LIVIA PLURABELLE

the way. [Hurry up and [17] slow you go. Give us the holy ashes here till I finish the canon's underpants.[18] Slow now. Slower still.]

First she let her hair fall and down it flowed to her [feet] and then mothernaked she washed herself [19] with bogwater and mudsoap from [her] crown to [her] sole. [Then she] greased [the groove of] her keel with butterscotch and multiplied [with leafmould brown islands] all over [her] little mary. Then she wove a garland for her hair. [She] pleated it. [She] plaited it. Of meadowgrass and riverflags, [of] bulrushes and waterweeds, [of] leaves of weeping willow. Then she made her bracelets and her anklets and her armlets [and an] amulet [for] necklet of [cobbles] and pebbles and rich gems and rare ones, [of] rhinestones and [watershellmarbles. That done] she sent her boudoir maid to Humphrey with a request that she might leave him for a moment and said she wouldn't be any length [away]. Then with her mealiebag [slung over] her shoulder, Anna Livia, oysterface, out at last she came.

Describe her! [Hurry up, why can't you?] [O] I must hear that! What had she on [the little old oddity]? What did she carry? Here she [is]. What has she got? A loin of jubilee [mountain] mutton?

[No mutton at all. I] tell you now but you must sit still. Will you hold your peace [and] listen well [20] to what I am going to say [now]. [It might have been 10 or 20 to 1] The door of the ugly igloo opened and out stepped a fairy woman [the dearest little mother ever you saw, nodding around her all smiles], the height of your knee. Go away! No more. The height of your knee. She wore a [ploughboy's] nailstudded [clogs, a pair of ploughfields in themselves]: a sugarloaf hat with a sunrise peak and a band of gorse and a golden pin [to pierce] it: [owlglassy [21] bicycles shaded] her eyes: [and a fishnet veil she had to keep the sun from spoiling her wrinkles]: potatorings buckled the loose ends of her ears: [her] nude cuba stockings were salmonspotspeckled: [she wore a shimmy of hazegrey: stout stays laced her length: her] bloodorange knickers showed natural nigger [boggers] fancy fastened [free to undo]:[22] her [blackstripe] tan joseph was teddybearlined [with a soft border of swansdown]: a [brace] of gaspers stuck in her hayrope garters: her civvy coat was [boundaried round] by a twobar [tunnel belt]: she had a clothespeg

TEXT B

tight astride of her nose and something [quaint that she held]²³ in her mouth and the tail of her [snuffdrab ²⁴ shiuler's] skirt trailed [40 Irish] miles behind her on the road.²⁵

O ²⁶ hellsbells,²⁷ I'm sorry I missed [her].²⁸ [Everyone who saw her said the sweet ²⁹ little lady seemed a bit queer. Funny poor dear she must have looked. There was a gang of surfacemen ³⁰ boomslanging and plugchewing, lying and leasing, on Lazy Wall and as soon as they seen who was in it ³¹ says one to the other: Between you and me and the wall beneath us ³² as round as a hoop Alp has doped] Dickens a funnier ever you saw.³³ But what was the game in her mixed bag? [Shake it up, do, do! and I promise I'll make it worth your while and I don't mean maybe. Tell me all. Tell me true] I want to get it while it's fresh. Well, she pattered around like Santa Claus with a Xmas box apiece for each and every one of her childer ³⁴ and they all around, [youths and maidens, stinkers and heelers, all her natural sons and daughters, 1001, chipping her] raising a [jeer or] cheer every time she'd dip in her [sack ³⁵ and out with her maundy money]. A tinker's tan and [a] bucket [to boil his billy] for Gipsy Lee: a cartridge of cockaleekie soup for Tommy the Soldier: for Pender's nephew acid drops [curiously strong]: a cough and a rattle and rosy cheeks for poor little Petite O'Hara: a jigsaw puzzle [of needles and pins and blankets and shins] between them for Isabel and Llewelyn Marriage: a [brazen nose and castiron mittens] ³⁶ for [Bubsy] ³⁷ Beg: ³⁸ waterlegs ³⁹ and gumboots [each] for Bully ⁴⁰ Hayes [and Hurricane Hartigan]: [the] ⁴¹ flag of the saints and stripes for Kevineen O'Dea: a puffpuff for Pudge Craig: a [night] marching hare for Toucher Doyle: a bladder ⁴² balloon for Mary Selina [Stakelum: and a putty spade to Larry the Puckaun: a hippo's head for Promoter Dunne: for Dora Hopeandwater ⁴³ a coolingdouche and a warmingpan: to Nancy Shannon a lucky Tuam brooch: oakwood beads for Holy Biddy: a prodigal heart in fatted halves for ⁴⁴ Buck Jones, the boy of Clonliffe:⁴⁵ for Kitty Coleraine of Buttermilk Lane a penny wise for her foolish pitcher: and a slate pencil for Elsie Oram to scratch her toby, doing her sums:⁴⁶ and a big drum for Billy Dunboyne: for Wally Meagher a couple of pairs of Blarney breeks: and salt lag and waterlag for ⁴⁷ Boy McCormick: a cross and

ANNA LIVIA PLURABELLE

a pile for Lucky Joe: My colonial! That was a bagful!] But what did she give to Una Ward and Peggy Quilty and Teasy Kieran and Ena Lappin and Philomena O'Farrell and Moira MacCabe?[48] She gave them all [a] moonflower[49] and a bloodstone [and a pint and a half of prunejuice]. To Izzy[50] [her youngest the vision of love][51] beyond her [years]. To Shem, her [eldest,[52] the vista of] life before his time.

[Throw us][53] the soap and tell me the rest. I could listen to more and more again. [That's what I call a tale of a tub] This is the life for me.

Well, you know or don't you know but every story has an end look, look,[54] the dusk is growing. [What time is it? It must be late. It's ages now since I or anyone last[55] saw Waterhouse's clock They took it asunder I heard them say. When will they reassemble it?] Wring out the clothes. Wring in the dusk. Will we spread them here? [Yes, we will.] Spread on your side and I'll spread mine on mine. Where are all her childer now? Some here, more [no more],[56] more again gone to the stranger. I've heard tell that same brooch of the Shannons was married into a family beyond the ocean. And all the Dunnes takes eights in hats. But all that's left now to the last of the Meaghers I'm told it's a kneebuckle and two buttons in the front. Do you tell me that now? I do, in troth. Is that the Dunboyne [on his] statue behind you there riding his high horse? That! Throw the cobwebs from your eyes, woman, and spread your linen proper. What is[57] but a blackberry growth. [Or the[58] grey mare ass them four old codgers[59] owns. Do you mean Tarpey and Lyons and Gregory? I do[60] the four codgers themselves and old Johnny MacDougal along with them] My sight is getting thick now with shadows about me. I'll go home slowly my way. So will I too by mine.

[But] She was the queer old [skeowska][61] anyhow, Anna Livia [twinkletoes]. And sure he was the queer old [buntz][62] too, [dear dirty Dumpling,[63] father of each and all of[64] us.] Hadn't he the seven wives. He had paps too, [large][65] and[66] soft [ones].[67] Ho,[68] Lord. Twins of his chest. Ho[69] Lord save us! And what all men.[70] [His tittering] Daughters of.[71]

Can't hear with the waters of. The[72] chittering waters of. Flittering bats and mice all bawk talk. Are you not gone ahome? [What

34

TEXT B

wrong Malone?] [73] Can't hear the bawk of bats, all the liffeying waters of. Old talk save us! [My feet won't move.] I feel as old as yonder elm. A tale told of Shaun [or] [74] Shem? [All] Livia's daughtersons. Dark hawks hear us. Night night. My [old] head falls. I feel as heavy as [yonder] stone. Tell me of John or Shaun? Who were Shem [and] [75] Shaun the living sons [or] [76] daughters of? Night now! Tell me, [tell me], elm. Nighty night! Tell me a tale of stone. Beside the rivering waters of, hither and thither waters of. Night! [77]

✶ ✶ ✶ TEXT C

O T E L L me all about Anna Livia! I want to hear all about Anna Livia. Well, you know Anna Livia? Yes, of course, we all know Anna Livia. Tell me all. Tell me now. You'll die when you hear. Well, you [know], when the old chap went [[phut]] and did what you know. Yes. I know, go on. Wash away and don't be dabbling. [Tuck up your sleeves and loosen your talktapes.] Or whatever it was they try to make out he tried to do in the Phoenix park. He's an awful old rep. Look at the shirt of him! Look at the dirt of it! [He has all my water black on me. And it steeping and stuping since this time last week.] [[How many times is it I wonder I washed it? I know by heart the places he likes to soil. Scorching my hand and starving my famine to make his private linen public. Wallop it well with your battle and clean it. My wrists are rusty rubbing the mouldy stains. And the loads of wet and the sewers of sin in it!]] [1] What [2] was it he did at all [[at all on Animal Sunday? And how long [3] was he under lough and neagh.]] It was put in the papers what he did. But time will tell. I [4] know it will. [Time and tide will wash for no man.] O, the [5] old old rep! [[And the cut of him! And the strut of him! How he used to hold his head as high as a howeth with a hump of grandeur on him like a walking rat]] What age is he at all at all? Or where was he born or how was he found and were him and her ever spliced? [[I heard he got some money with her when he brought [6] her home in a perokeet's cage, the quaggy way for stumbling.[7] Who sold [8] you that jackalantern's tale? In a gabbard he landed, the boat of life, and he loosed two

NOTE: This text is a transcription of the first typescript; emendations in the preceding fair copy are indicated by single brackets; emendations in the typescript are indicated by double brackets.

TEXT C

croakers from under his tilt, the old Phenician rover. By the smell of her kelp they made the pigeonhouse.]] Don't you know he's a bairn of the sea, Waterhouse the waterbaby? O, I know, so he was. H.C.E. has [a cockly] ee. Sure she's nearly as bad as him [9] herself. Who? Anna Livia? Ay, Anna Livia. Do you know she was calling girls [from all around] to go in [till him], [[her erring man]], and tickle him [easy]? She was? Go to God! O, tell me all I want to hear. Letting on she didn't care, [[the proxenete! Proxenete and what is that? Were you never at school? It's just the same as if I was to go for example now and proxenete you. For God' sake and is that what she is?]] Didn't you [spot] her in her windeye, [standing up on a rickety chair], pretending to [[ripple]] [10] a tune or two [on] a fiddle she has without a bottom? Sure she can't [fiddledeedee, top or bottom]! Of course, she can't! All a blind. Well, I never heard the like of that! Tell me more. Tell me all.

Well, old [Humber] was as [11] glum as a grampus, [setting] moping on his benk, hunger striking [all alone, and] holding [doomsdag] over himself, dreeing his weird, with his dander up, [and] his [[fringe]] [12] combed over his [eygs] and keeking on loft [till] the face [of] the sternes. [[You'd think all was dead belonging to him. He had been belching for over a year.]] And there she was, Anna Livia, she couldn't snatch a wink of sleep, [purling] around like a [chit of a child], in a short summer skirt and painted cheeks. And an odd time she'd cook him up blooms of fisk [13] and [[lay at his feet her]] meddery [eygs and] [[beacons on toask]] [shinking bread for] to plaise [that [14] man hog] stay his [stomicker], and as [rash] as she'd [[rush]] with them up on [her] tray the old chap'd cast them from him, with a scowl [of scorn, as much as to say you this and you that, and] if he didn't peg the tea in her face, believe me, she was safe enough. And then she'd try to [fistle] a tune, *The Heart Bowed Down* or *The Rakes of Mallow*.[15] What harm if she knew how [16] to cock her mouth. And not a mag out of him no more than [[out of the mangle weight]]. Is that a fact? That's a fact. And cheeping to him down the feedchute, with all kinds of fondling endings, the [poother rambling] off [17] her nose: Vuggybarney, Wickerymandy! Hello, ducky, please don't die! [18] Do you know what she started singing

ANNA LIVIA PLURABELLE

then, [the] voice [of] her like a water gluck? You'll never guess. Tell me. Tell me. *Phoebe, dearest, tell, O tell me* and *I loved you better [nor] you knew*. And letting on she was daft about the [warbly [19] sangs] from over [holmen]: *High hellskirt saw ladies [hensmoker] lilyhung pigger* [[and himself below as deaf as a yawn]]. Go away! [You're only jeering!] Anna [Liv]? As God is my judge! And didn't she [up and rise and] go and trot down and stand in the door, [[puffing her old dudheen]] and every country wench [or] farmerette [walking] the [roads] usedn't she make her a sign to slip inside by the [sallypost]?[20] You don't say the sallyport? I did. I do. Calling them [in][21] one by one and legging a jig or two to show them how to shake their benders and the dainty how to bring to mind the gladdest garments out of sight and all the way of a maid with a man and making a [sort] of a cackling noise like two and a penny or half a crown and holding up a silver shiner. Lordy, lordy, [did she so]? Well, of all the ones ever I heard! Throwing all the girls [of] the world at him! To any lass [you like] of no matter what sex of playful ways two and a tanner a girl a go to [hug] and have fun in Humpy's lap!

And what about the rhyme she made! O that! Tell me that [while I'm lathering hell out of Denis Florence MacCarthy's combies]. I'm dying down off my feet until I hear Anna Livia's rhyme! I can see that, I see you are. How does it go? Listen now. [Are you listening? Yes, yes! Indeed I am! Listen now. Listen in:]

By earth and heaven but I badly want a brandnew backside, bedad and I do, and a plumper at that!

For the putty affair I have is [wore] out, so it is, sitting, yawning and waiting for my old Dane the dodderer, my life in death companion, my frugal key of [our] larder, my muchaltered camel's hump, my jointspoiler, my maymoon's honey, my fool to the last Decemberer, to wake [himself] out of his winter's doze and shout me down like he used to.

Is there a lord of the manor or [a] knight of the shire at all, I wonder, that'd tip me a pound or two in cash for washing and darning his worshipful socks for him now we're run out of horsemeat and milk?

Only for my featherbed is as snug as it smells it's out I'd lep and off with me to the [slobs] of the Tolka or[22] *the Bull of Clontarf to*

TEXT C

[[*hear*]] *the gay air of my* [[*salt*]] *Dublin bay and the race of the seawind up my hole.*

O go on! Tell me more. Tell me every tiny bit. I want to [know] every single thing. Well, now comes the [[hatchery]] part. How many [[aleveens]] [had] she at all? I can't rightly tell you that. God only [knows]. [Some] say she had a hundred and eleven. She can't remember half [[of]] the [[cradlenames]] she [[smacked]] on them [[by the grace of her boxing bishop's infallible slipper]]. A hundred and how? They did [well] to christen her Plurabelle.[23] O laws! What a flock! She must have been a gadabout in her day, so she must, more than most. So she was, you bet! [[She had a flewmen of her owen.]] Tell me, tell me, how did she come through all her fellows, the daredevil? Who was the first that ever burst? Someone it was, whoever you are. Tinker, tailor, soldier, sailor, Paul Pry or polishman. That's the thing I always want to know.[24] She can't put her hand on him for the moment. [It's a long long way, walking weary![25] Such a [26] long way backwards to go!] She says herself she hardly [knows] who [her graveller] was or what he did [or how young she was] or when [and where and how often] he crossed her. She was just a young thin pale [soft shy slim] slip of a thing then, sauntering,[27] and he was a heavy [trudging] lurching lieabroad [of a] Curraghman, making [his] hay for the sun to shine [on], as [tough][28] as the [oaktrees] used to [rustle] that time [down by the dykes of] killing [29] Kildare, that first fell [with a plash] across her. [[She thought she'd sink under the ground with shame!]] You're wrong there, all wrong! It was ages long before that in county Wicklow, the garden of Erin, before she ever dreamt she'd [[leave Kilbride and go roaring under Horsepass bridge to]] end [her days] in the barleyfields and pennylands of Humphrey's [fordofhurdlestown] and lie with a landleaper, well on the wane. Was it? Was it? Are you sure?[30] Where in Wicklow? Tell me where, the very first time! I will if you listen. You know the hazel dell of Luggelaw? Well, there once dwelt a local hermit, Michael [[Arklow]][31] [was his name], and one day in [burning] June so [sweet] and [so fresh] and so limber she looked, the kind of curves you simply can't stop feeling, he plunged both of his blessed anointed hands up to his wrists in the [singing [32] saffron] streams of her hair, [parting

39

ANNA LIVIA PLURABELLE

them and soothing her and mingling it],[33] that was [deepred and ample] like the brown bog [at sundown]. And he couldn't [34] help [himself], thirst was too hot for him, he had to forget the monk in the man [so, rubbing her up and smoothing her down], he cooled his lips in smiling mood, kiss after kiss, [[(as he warned her never to, never to, never)]] on Anna Livia's freckled [forehead]. O, wasn't he the bold priest? And wasn't she the naughty Livvy? Naughty-naughty [35] is her name. Two lads in their breeches went through her before that, Barefoot [[Burn]] [36] and Billy Wade, Lugnaquilla's noble pair, before she had a hint of a hair there to hide and ere that again she was licked by a hound while doing her pee, sweet and simple, on the [slope] of [a] hill [in] old Kippure in birdsong and shearingtime but first of all, worst of all, she sideslipped [37] out by a gap in the Devil's Glen [while] [[Sally]] her nurse was sound asleep in a sloot and fell [over a spillway] [38] before she found her stride and lay and wriggled [in all the stagnant black pools of rain] [39] under a fallow cow, [laughing free with her limbs aloft, and a whole drove of maiden hawthorns blushing and looking askance upon her].

Tell me the sound of the shorthorn's name. And tell me why the something was she freckled. And tell me too how long was her hair or was it only a wig she wore. Are you in this game or are you not? O go on, go on, go on! I mean about what you know. I know [[right]] well what you mean. [What am I [40] rinsing now and I'll thank you? Is it a pinny or is it a surplice? Arrah, where's your nose? And where's the starch? That's not the benediction [41] smell. I can tell from here by the *eau de Cologne* and the scent of her moisture they're Mrs Magrath's.] [[And you ought to have aired them. They've just come off her. Creases of silk they are, not crimps of lawn. The only pair with frills in all the land.]] [42] [So they are. Well, well!] [[And there is [43] her maiden letters too. Ell and a quay in scarlet thread. And an ex after to show they're not Laura Kelly's. O, may the devil twist your [44] safety pin!]] [Now [45] who has been tearing the leg of her drawers on her? Which leg is it? The one with the bells on it. Rinse them [46] out and run along with you!] Where did I stop? [Never] stop. Continuation. You're not there yet. Go on, go on!

Well, after it was put in the Beggar's [Monday] Journal [[even the

TEXT C

snow that fell on his hoaring hair had a skunner against him]]. Everywhere [47] ever you went and every bung you ever dropped [48] into or wherever you scoured the countryside you found his picture upside down or the cornerboys [49] burning his guy and Pat [50] the Man reeling and rolling around the local with oddfellow's triple tiara busby rotundarinking round his scalp. So she said to herself she'd make a plan to make a shine, the mischiefmaker, the like of it you never heard. What plan? Tell me quickly. What the mischief did she do? Well, she borrowed a bag, a mailbag, [off] one of her sons,[51] Shaun the Post, and then she went and made herself up. O God of gigglers.[52] I can't tell [you] how! It's too screaming funny, rabbit it all! O but you must, you must really! By the holy well of Mulhuddart I swear I'd give my chance of going to heaven to hear it all, every word. [[O, leave me my faculties, woman, a while. If you don't like my story get out of the boat. Well, have [53] it your own way, so]] Here, sit down and do as you're [bid]. Go easy [and] keep quiet. Tell me slow. Take your time now. Breathe deep. That's the way. Hurry up and slow you go. Give us [your] holy ashes here till I [scrub] the canon's underpants. Slow now. Slower still.

First she let her hair fall and down it flowed to her feet.[54] Then, mothernaked, she washed herself with bogwater and mudsoap, [[upper and lower]], from crown to sole.[55] [Next] she greased the groove of her keel with [[antifouling]] butterscotch and with leafmould [she] multiplied [a thousand isles and islets dun] all over her little mary. [And after that] she wove a garland for her hair. She pleated it. She plaited it. Of meadowgrass and riverflags, [the bulrush] and [waterweed, and] of [fallen] leaves of [56] weeping willow. Then she made her bracelets and her anklets and her armlets and [a [57] jetty] amulet for [necklace] of [clicking] cobbles and [pattering] pebbles,[58] [and [59] rumbledown [60] rubble], rich gems and [61] rare, of [Irish] rhinestones [and shellmarble bangles]. That done, she sent her boudoir maid to [[His Affluence]] with [[respects from his missus, seepy and sewery, and]] a request she might leave him for a moment. [[She]] said she wouldn't be any length away. Then, [then], with her mealiebag slung over her shoulder, Anna Livia, oysterface, out at last she came.

ANNA LIVIA PLURABELLE

Describe her! [Bustle along], why can't you? [[Spit on the iron while it's hot. I wouldn't miss her for the world.]] I must, [I absolute must] hear that! What had she on the little old oddity? [How much] did she carry [[harness and weights]]? Here she is, [[Amnisty Ann. Call her calamity electrifies man.]] [62]

No [[electress]] at all. [I'll] tell you now. But you must sit still. Will you hold your peace and listen well to what I am going to say now? It might have been ten or twenty to one [when] the door of [her] ugly igloo opened and out stepped a fairy woman, the dearest little mother ever you saw, nodding around her, all smiles, [[between two ages]], [a judyqueen], the height of your knee. [And look at her sharp and seize her quick for the longer she lives the shorter she grows.] Go away! No more? [63] [[Why where did you ever see a lambloin chop as big as a battering ram? Ay, you're right. I was forgetting]] The height of your knee, [[I say]]! She wore a ploughboy's nailstudded clogs, a pair of ploughfields in themselves: a sugarloaf hat with a sunrise peak and a band of gorse [and a hundred streamers dancing off it] and a golden pin to pierce it: owlglassy bicycles [boggled] her eyes: and a fishnet veil she had to keep the sun from spoiling her wrinkles: potatorings buckled the loose ends of her ears: her nude cuba stockings were salmonspotspeckled:[64] she [sported] a shimmy of hazegrey [[that once was blue till it ran in the washing]]:[65] stout stays, [[the rivals]], [lined] her length: her bloodorange knickers showed natural nigger boggers, fancy fastened, free to undo: her blackstripe tan joseph was teddybearlined, with [wavy grassgreen epaulettes] [[and]] a border [here and there] of swansdown: a brace of gaspers stuck in her hayrope garters: her civvy coat was boundaried round [with] a twobar tunnel belt: she had a clothespeg tight astride of her nose and [she kept on grinding] something quaint [66] in her mouth and the tail of her snuffdrab [shuiler's] skirt trailed forty Irish miles behind her on the road.

Hellsbells, I'm sorry I missed her! [[But in which of her mouths? Was her nose alight?]] Everyone [that] saw her said the [douce] little lady [looked] a bit queer. Funny poor [frump] she must have looked. Dickens a funnier ever you saw. [[Well [67] for her she couldn't see herself.]] There was a gang of [drouthdropping] surfacemen, boom-

TEXT C

slanging and plugchewing, [[lolling]] and leasing on Lazy Wall and as soon as they [saw her trip by in profile and twigged] who [it was was] in it, [Lucan's fish and Dublin's poison], says one to another: Between [me and you] and the [granite we're warming] as round as a hoop Alp has doped.

But what was the game in her mixed bag? I want to get it while it's fresh. [[I bet my beard it's worth while poaching on.]] Shake it up, do, do!⁶⁸ I promise I'll make it worth your while. And I don't mean maybe. Tell me [what and] tell me true.

Well, around she pattered [and swung and sidled not knowing which way to turn] like Santa Claus [[at the call of the pale and puny]] with a Christmas box apiece for each and everyone⁶⁹ of her childer⁷⁰ and they all [about her], youths and maidens, chipping her, [and] raising [a bit of] a jeer or cheer every time she'd dip in her sack [of rubbish she robbed] and [reach out]⁷¹ her maundy [merchandise], stinkers and heelers, [laggards and primeboys] all her natural sons and daughters, a thousand and one [of them, and something for each of them]. A tinker's tan and a bucket to boil his billy for Gipsy Lee: a cartridge of cockaleekie⁷² soup for Tommy the Soldier: for [sulky] Pender's [[acid]] nephew [[deltoid]] drops,⁷³ curiously strong: a cough and a rattle and [wildrose] cheeks for poor little Petite⁷⁴ O'Hara: a jigsaw puzzle of needles and pins and blankets and shins between them for Isabel and Llewelyn Marriage: a brazen nose and [pigiron] mittens⁷⁵ for [Johnny Walker] Beg: the [papal] flag of the saints and stripes for Kevineen O'Dea: a puffpuff for Pudge Craig [and] a nightmarching hare for Toucher Doyle: [waterleg]⁷⁶ and gumboots each for Bully Hayes and Hurricane Hartigan:⁷⁷ a prodigal heart [and] fatted [calves] for Buck Jones, the [pride] of Clonliffe: [a loaf of bread and a father's early kick for Tim from Skibereen: a jauntingcar for Larry Doolin, the Ballyclee jackeen:⁷⁸ a seasick⁷⁹ trip on a government ship for Peat O'Flanagan: a louse and trap for Jerry Coyle: mudmincepies for Andy Mackenzie:⁸⁰ a hairclip⁸¹ and clackdish for Penceless Peter: a spellingbee book for Rosy Brooke:]⁸² [[a drowned doll for Sister Anne:]] [scruboak] beads for holy⁸³ Biddy: [[an applewood stool for Eva Thornstone: for Sara Philpot a jordan valley tearjar:]] [a pretty box

ANNA LIVIA PLURABELLE

of Pettyfib's powder for Eileen Alannah [84] to whiten her teeth: a whipping top for Eddy Lawless:] for Kitty Coleraine of Buttermilk Lane a penny wise for her foolish pitcher: a putty [shovel for] Larry the Puckaun: a [potamus] [[mask]] for Promoter Dunne: [[a dynamite egg for Paul the Curate:]] [85] a pile [with] a cross [on the back] for [Sunny Jim: for] Nancy Shannon a Tuam brooch: for Dora Hopeandwater a coolingdouche [86] and a warmingpan: a [pair] of Blarney breeks for Wally Meagher: a [hairpin] slatepencil for Elsie Oram to scratch her toby, doing her [best with her] [[volgar]] [fractions]: [[an old age pension for Betty the Beauty: a bag of the blues for Funny Fitz: Jill,[87] the spoon of a girl, for Jack, the broth of a boy: a Robinson Crusoe Friday fast for Patrick Angelus Rubinstein: three [88] hundred and sixtysix poplin ties for everyday in the annual year for Victor Hugonot:[89] a rake and good [90] muck for Kate the Cleaner: a hole in the ballad for Hosty: two dozen of cradles for [91] J.F.X.P. Coppinger: a letter to last a lifetime for Maggy beyond by the ashpit: the heaviest deaf and dumb woman from Lusk to Livienbad [92] for Felim the Ferry: spas [93] and speranza for gouty Gough: a sunless map of the world including the moon and stamp [94] for Shaun the Post: a stonecold shoulder for Donn Joe Vance: a lock and a stable for Honorbright [95] Meretrix:]] a big drum for Billy Dunboyne: [[Whatever you like to take to drink for Festus King and Roaring Peter and Frisky Shorty and Treacle Tom and Maurice Behan and Sully the Thug and Master Magrath and Peter Cloran and whoever you [96] chance to meet knocking around:]] [and] a bladder balloon for [97] Selina [[Susquehana]] Stakelum. But what did she give to [[Pruda]] Ward and Peggy Quilty [and Nora Brosna] [98] and Teasy Kieran and Ena Lappin [99] [[and Una and Bina and Trina Kane]] and Philomena O'Farrell [and Josephine Foyle] [[and Lily and Laura]] [100] and [Mary Xavier Agnes] [[Daisy]] [Francis de Sales] MacCabe? She gave them [every mother's daughter] a moonflower and a bloodstone. [And] to Izzy, her youngest, [a] vision of love beyond her [years and] to Shem, her eldest, life before his time.

My colonial, [what] a bagful! That's what [you may] call a tale of a tub. [[No wonder they'd run from her like the plague]] Throw us the soap [for the honour of God]. [[The wee bit the water left.]]

TEXT C

[You've all the swirls your side of the current. Well, am I to blame for that if I have? Who said you're to blame for that if you have? [101] My hands are as blue between cold and soda as that piece of pattern chayney there, lying below. Or where is it? Lying beside the reeds I saw it.] [[With that peaty water who could see?]] [But O, go on. I love a gabber.] [102] I could listen to more and more again. [Rain on [103] the river. Flies to your float.] [104] This is the life for me.

Well, you know or don't you know [or haven't I told you] every story has an end. Look, look, the dusk is growing. What time is it? It must be late. It's ages now [105] since I or anyone last saw Waterhouse's clock. They took it asunder, I heard them say. When will they reassemble it? [[O, my back, my back, my back!]] Wring out the clothes! Wring in the [dew]! Will we spread them here [now? Ay], we will. Spread on your [bank] and I'll spread mine on mine. [It's what I'm doing. Spread! It's turning chill.[106] A wind is rising. I'll lay [107] a few stones on the hotel sheets. A man and his bride embraced [108] between them.] [[Else I'd have sprinkled and folded them only.]] [109] [And I'll tie my butcher's apron here.] [[It's suety yet. The strollers will pass it by.]] [110] [Six shifts, ten kerchiefs, the convent [111] napkins [112] twelve, one baby's shawl.] Where are all her childer now? Some here, more no more, more again [lost] to the stranger.[113] I've heard tell that same brooch of the Shannons was married into a family [114] [in Spain]. And all the Dunnes [115] [[beyond Brendan's sea]] takes [number nine] in hats. [And one of Biddy's beads went [116] bobbing [117] till she rounded up [118] last Friday week with a marigold and a cobbler's candle in a main drain off Bachelor's Walk.] But all that's left to the last of the Meaghers [119] [is one] kneebuckle and two [hooks] in the front. Do you tell me that now? I do, in troth. Is that the [great] Dunboyne [himself] on his statue riding his high horse there [fornenst] you? [There? Is it] that? [[On Fallareen [120] Common.]] [121] Throw the cobwebs from your eyes, woman, and spread your [washing] proper. [[It's well I know your sort of slop. Were you lifting your elbow, tell us, glazy cheeks, in the Carrigacurra canteen. Was I what hobbledehips? Amn't I up since the damp dawn with varicose veins, soaking and bleaching boiler rags, and sweating cold, a widow like me, to deck my tennis champion son, the laundryman

45

ANNA LIVIA PLURABELLE

with the lavender flannels? Holy St. Wolstan, I saw it again! Near the golden falls. There! Subdue your noise, you poor creature!]] [122] What is [it] but a blackberry [123] growth [124] or the grey mare ass them four old codgers owns. [Are] you [meaning] Tarpey and Lyons and Gregory? I [mean those] four codgers that [125] [owns that stray in the mist] [126] and old Johnny MacDougal along with them. [Is that the Poolbeg [127] flasher [128] beyond or the mast of a coaster near [129] the Kish or a glow I behold within a hedge?] [[Wait till the rising of the moon.]] My sight is getting [thicker on me] with [the] shadows [in this place]. I'll go home slowly [now] my [own] way, [the valley way]. So will I too by mine.

[Ah], but she was the queer old [skeowsha] [130] anyhow,[131] Anna Livia, twinkletoes! And sure he was the queer old buntz [132] too, Dear Dirty [133] Dumpling, [foostherfather] of all of us. [Gammer and gaffer we're all their gangsters.[134] Hadn't he seven dams to wive him? And every dam [135] had her seven crutches. And every crutch had [136] its seven hues. And each [137] hue had a different cry. Suds for me and supper for you and the doctor's bill for John Joe.] [138] [[Before! Before! He married his markets, cheap by foul,[139] I know, but at milkingmass [140] who was the spouse? Then all that was was fair. Teems of times and happy returns. The same anew.]] He had [buckgoat] [141] paps [on him], [142] soft ones [for orphans]. Ho, Lord! Twins of his [bosom]. Lord save us. And [ho! Hey?] [143] What all men. [Hot?] [144] His tittering daughters of. [Whawk?]

Can't hear with the waters of. The chittering waters of. Flittering bats, [fieldmice] bawk talk. [Ho!] Are you not gone ahome? [What Tom] Malone? Can't hear [with] bawk of bats, all the liffeying waters of. [Ho], talk save us! My [foos woon't [145] moos]. I feel as old [146] as yonder elm. A tale told of Shaun or Shem? All [147] Livia's daughter-sons. Dark hawks hear us! Night! Night! My [ho] head [halls]. I feel as heavy as yonder stone. Tell me of John or Shaun? Who were Shem and Shaun the living sons or daughters of? Night now! Tell me, tell me, [tell me], elm! [[Night]] [148] night! Tell me tale of [stem or] stone. Beside the rivering waters of, [hitherandthithering] waters of. Night! [149]

ꝶ ꝶ ꝶ ꝶ TEXT D

O TELL me all about Anna Livia! I want to hear all about Anna Livia. Well, you know Anna Livia? Yes, of course, we all know Anna Livia. Tell me all. Tell me now. You'll die when you hear. Well, you know, when the old chap went [[futt]] and did what you know. Yes, I know, go on. Wash away and don't be dabbling. Tuck up your sleeves and loosen your talktapes. Or whatever it was they try to make out he tried to do in the [[[Fiendish]]] park. He's an awful old rep. Look at the shirt of him! Look at the dirt of it! He has all my water black on me. And it steeping and stuping since this time last week. How many times is it I wonder I washed it? I know by heart the places he likes to soil. Scorching my hand and starving my famine to make his private linen public. Wallop it well with your battle and clean it. My wrists are rusty rubbing the [[mouldaw]] stains. And the [[dneepers]] of wet and the [[gangres]] of sin in it! What was it he did at all at all on Animal Sunday? And how long was he under lough and neagh. It was put in the papers what he did, [[illysus distilling and all]]. But time will tell. I know it will. Time and tide will wash for no man. O, the old old rep! And the cut of him! And the strut of him! How he used to hold his head high as a howeth, [[[the famous old duke alien]]], with a hump of grandeur on him like a walking rat. What age is he at all at all? Or where was he born or how was he found and were him and her ever spliced? I heard he [[dug good tin]] with [[his doll]],[1] when he brought her home, [[[Sabine asthore]]], in a

NOTE: This text is a composite of the *Calendar* galleys and, where these are deficient, the typescript from which they were set. Emendations on the partial second typescript are enclosed in single brackets, those on the third copy of the third typescript in double brackets, those on the galleys in triple brackets.

ANNA LIVIA PLURABELLE

[[[parakeet's]]] ² cage, the quaggy way for stumbling. Who sold you that jackalantern's tale? In a gabbard he landed, the boat of life, and he loosed two croakers from under his tilt, the old Phenician rover. By the smell of her kelp they made the pigeonhouse. [[Like fun they did but where was Himself? ³ That ⁴ [[[marchantman]]] ⁵ he follied their scutties right over the wash, his cameleer's burnous breezing up on him, till with his runagate bowmpriss he rode and borst ⁶ her bar. Pwllhyllyou! ⁷ Och, I'm kilt! Tune your pipes and fall ahumming, you born ijypt,⁸ and you're nothing short of one! ⁹ When they saw him shoot swift ¹⁰ up her sheba sheath, like any gay lord salomon,¹¹ her bulls they were roaring, surfed with spree. Nooknoorum nyroo! Nooknoorum nyroo! He erned ¹² his lille Bunbath ¹³ hard,¹⁴ our staly bred, the trader. He did. Look at here. In this wet of his prow.]] Don't ¹⁵ you know [[he was]] a bairn of the sea, Waterhouse the waterbaby? O, I know, so he was. H.C.E. has a [[briny]] ee. Sure she's nearly as bad as him herself. Who? Anna Livia? Ay, Anna Livia. Do you know she was calling [backwater] girls from all around, to go in till him, her erring man, and tickle [[the pontiff]] easy? She was? Go to [[pot]]! O, tell me all I want to hear. Letting on she didn't care, the proxenete! Proxenete and [[phwhat]] ¹⁶ is [[phthat? Did they never otter]] you [[ebro]] at ¹⁷ [[skol]]? It's just the same as if I was to go for example now and proxenete you. For [[cox']] ¹⁸ sake and is that what she is? Didn't you spot her in her windeye, [[wubbling]] up on [[[an osiery]]] ¹⁹ chair, pretending to [[ribble]] a [[reedy derg]] ²⁰ on a fiddle she [[bows]] without a bottom? Sure she can't [[fiddan a dee, bow]] or bottom! [[Srue]], she can't. [[Just a suck.]] Well, I never heard the like of that! Tell me more. Tell me [[[most]]]. Well, old Humber was as glum as a grampus, setting moping on his benk, [where he'd check their [[[debths]]] ²¹ in that mormon's thames], hungerstriking all alone and holding doomsdag over himself,²² dreeing his weird, with his dander up, and his fringe combed over his eygs and keeking on loft till the [sight] of the sternes. You'd think all was dead belonging to him. He had been belching for [[severn years]]. And there she was, Anna Livia, she [[darent catch a winkle]] of sleep, purling around like a chit of a child, in a [Lapsummer] skirt and [[[damazon]]]

TEXT D

cheeks. And an odd time she'd cook him up blooms of fisk and lay [[to]] [23] his [heartsfoot] her meddery eygs and [staynish] beacons on [toasc] [[and a cupenhave of Greenland's tay]] [and a] shinking bread for to plaise that man hog stay his stomicker [till her [[[pyrraknees shrunk]]] [24] to nutmeggraters] and as rash as she'd rush with [[her peakload of vivers]] up on her tray [[my bold Hek he'd kast]] them from him, with a [[stour]] of scorn, as much as to say you this and you that, and if he didn't peg the [plateau] in her face, believe me, she was safe enough. And then she'd try to [vistule] a [hymn], *The Heart Bowed Down* or *The Rakes of Mallow*. What harm if she knew how [25] to [[cockle]] her mouth! And not a mag out of [[Hum]] no more than out of the mangle weight. Is that a [[faith]]? That's a fact. And [[brahming]] to him down the feedchute, with all kinds of fondling endings, the poother rambling off her nose: *Vuggybarney, Wickerymandy! Hello, ducky, please don't die!* Do you know what she started [[cheeping]] then, the voice of her like a watergluck? You'll never guess. Tell me. Tell me. *Phoebe, dearest, tell, O tell me* and *I loved you better nor you knew*. And letting on she was daft about the warbly sangs from over holmen: *High hellskirt saw ladies hensmoker lilyhung pigger*: and [[[Oom Bothar]]] below [[[in his sandy cloak]]], as deaf as a yawn. Go away! You're only jeering! Anna Liv? As [[chalk]] is my judge! And didn't she up and rise and go and trot down and stand in the door, puffing her old dudheen, and every country wench or farmerette walking the [[pilend]] roads, usedn't she make her a sign to slip inside by the [[sullyport]]? You don't say, the [[sillypost]]? I did. [[And]] I do.[26] Calling them in one by one and legging a jig or [[[so]]] to show them how to shake their benders and the dainty how to bring to mind the gladdest garments out of sight and all the way of a maid with a man and making a sort of a cackling noise like two and a penny or half a crown and holding up a silver shiner. Lordy, lordy, did she so? Well, of all the ones ever I heard! Throwing all the girls of the world at him! To any lass you like of no matter what sex of playful ways two and a tanner a girl a go to hug and have fun in Humpy's [[apron]]!

And what [[was]] the [[wyerye]] [27] rhyme she made! O that! Tell me that while I'm [28] lathering hell out of Denis Florence MacCarthy's

ANNA LIVIA PLURABELLE

combies. I'm dying down off my [[iodine]] feet until I hear **Anna Livia's** [[cushingloo]]! I can see that, I see you are. How does it go? Listen now. Are you listening? Yes, yes! Indeed I am! Listen now. Listen in:

By earth and heaven but I badly want a brandnew [[bankside, bedamp]] [29] *and I do, and a plumper at that!*

For the putty affair I have is wore out, so it is, sitting, [[yaping]] and waiting for my old Dane the dodderer, my life in death companion, my frugal key of our larder, my muchaltered camel's hump, my jointspoiler, my maymoon's honey, my fool to the last Decemberer, to wake himself out of his winter's doze and shout me down like he used to.

Is there a lord of the manor or a knight of the shire at all, I wonder, that'd tip me a pound or two in cash for washing and darning his worshipful socks for him now we're run out of horsemeat and milk?

Only for my [[short Brittas bed is]] as snug as it smells it's out I'd lep and off with me to the slobs of the Tolka or the [[shores]] [30] *of Clontarf to hear the gay air of my salt [[troublin]] bay and the race of the [[saywint]] up [[me]] [[[ambushure]]].* [31]

O go on! Tell me more. Tell me every tiny bit. I want to know every single thing. Well, now comes the [[hazelhatchery]] part. How many aleveens had she [[in]] all? I can't rightly tell you that. [[Close]] only knows. Some say she had a hundred and eleven. She can't remember half of the cradlenames she smacked on them by the grace of her boxing bishop's infallible slipper. A hundred and how? They did well to [[rechristen]] her Plurabelle. O [[loreley!]] What a [[lots]]! She must have been a gadabout in her day, so she must, more than most. [[Shoal]] she was, you bet! She had a flewmen of her owen. Tell me, tell me, how [[could]] she [cam] through all her fellows, the daredevil? [Linking one and knocking the next, and [[[palling]]] [32] in and [[[petering]]] [33] out and clyding by on her eastway.] [34] Who was the first that ever burst? Someone it was, whoever you are. Tinker, tailor, soldier, sailor, Paul Pry or polishman. That's the thing I always want to know. She can't put her hand on him for the moment. It's a long long way, walking weary! Such a long way backwards to [[row]]! She says herself she hardly knows who her grav-

TEXT D

eller was or what he did or how young she [[played]] or when and where and how often he [[jumped]] her. She was just a young thin pale soft shy slim slip of a thing then, sauntering, and he was a heavy trudging lurching lieabroad of a Curraghman, making his hay for the sun to shine on, as tough as the oaktrees [[(peats be with them!)]] used to rustle that time down by the dykes of killing Kildare, that [forstfellfoss] with a plash across her. She thought she'd sink under the ground with shame [[[when he gave her the tigris eye]]]! You're wrong there, [[[corribly]]] [35] wrong! It was ages [behind] that [when nullahs were nowhere], in county [[Wickenlow]], garden of Erin, before she ever dreamt she'd leave Kilbride and go [fuming] under Horsepass bridge to [[wend]] her [[ways byandby]], [rebecca or worse], in the barleyfields and [[[pennylotts]]] of Humphrey's fordofhurdlestown and lie with a landleaper,[36] [[wellingtonorseher. Wasut? Izod?]] Are you [[suir]]?[37] [[Whereabouts in Ow and Ovoca?]] [Was it north by south or Lucan Yokan[38] or where the hand of man has never set foot?] Tell me where, the very first time! I will if you listen. You know the [dingley] dell of Luggelaw? Well, there once dwelt a local [[heremite]] Michael Arklow was his name, [[(with many a sigh I aspersed his lavabibs!)]] and one [[venersderg]][39] in [[junojuly]] so sweet and so fresh and so limber she looked, the kind of curves you simply can't stop feeling, he plunged both of his blessed anointed hands up to his wrists in the singing saffron streams of her hair, parting them and soothing her and mingling it, that was deepred and ample like the [[[red]]] bog at sundown. And he couldn't help himself, [[thurst]] was too hot [[on]] him, he had to forget the monk in the man so, rubbing her up and smoothing her down, he cooled his lips in smiling mood, kiss after kiss (as he warned her never to, never to, never) on Anna Livia's freckled forehead. O, wasn't he the bold priest? And wasn't she the naughty Livvy? Naughty [[Naama]] is her name. Two[40] lads in their breeches went through her before that, Barefoot Burn and [[Willy]] Wade, [[Lugnaquillia's]] noble pair, before she had a hint of a hair [[at her fanny]] to hide and ere that again she was licked by a hound, while [[poing]] her pee, [[pure]][41] and simple, on[42] the [[spur]] of [[the]] hill in old Kippure in birdsong and shearingtime, but first of all, worst

ANNA LIVIA PLURABELLE

of all, she sideslipped out by a gap in the Devil's glen while Sally her nurse was sound asleep in a sloot and fell over a spillway before she found her stride and lay and wriggled in all the stagnant black pools of rain under a fallow cow [[and she laughed innocefree]] with her limbs aloft and a whole drove of maiden hawthorns blushing and looking askance upon her.

[[Drop]] me the sound of the shorthorn's name. And [[drip]] me why [[in]] the something was she freckled. And [[trickle]] [43] me [[through was she marcelwaved]] or was it [[weirdly]] [44] a wig she wore. Are you in [[the swim]] or are you [[out]]? O go on, go on, go on! I mean about what you know. I know right well what you mean. What am I rinsing now and I'll thank you? Is it a pinny or is it a surplice? [[Arran]], where's your nose? And where's the starch? That's not the benediction smell. I can tell from here by [[their]] *eau de* [[*Niels*]] and the scent of her moisture they're Mrs Magrath's. And you ought to have aired them. They've just come off her. Creases [[in]] silk they are, not [[crampton]] lawn. The only pair with frills in [[old]] the [[plain]]. So they are. Well, well! And there is her [[nubilee]] letters too. [[Ellis on]] quay in scarlet thread. And an ex after to show they're not Laura [[Kehoe's]]. O, may [45] the devil twist your safety pin! Now who has been tearing the leg of her drawers on her? Which leg is it? The one with the bells on it. Rinse them out and [[aston]] along with you. Where did I stop? Never stop. [[Continuarration.]] You're not there yet. [[Garonne, garonne!]]

Well, after it was put in the Beggar's Monday [46] Journal, even the snow that fell on his hoaring hair had a skunner against him. Everywhere ever you went and every bung you ever dropped into or wherever you scoured the countryside [[from Nannywater to Vartryville]] you found his [[picture]] [47] upside down or the cornerboys [48] burning his guy and Pat the Man reeling and rolling around the local with oddfellow's triple tiara busby rotundarinking round his scalp. [[She swore she'd be level with all of them yet.]] So she said to herself she'd [[frame]] [49] a plan to [[fake]] a shine, the mischiefmaker, the like of it you never heard. What plan? Tell me quickly. What the mischief did she [[make]]? Well, she [[bergened]] a bag, a [[shammy]] mailbag, off one of her [[swapsons]], Shaun the Post, and then she went

TEXT D

and made herself up. O [[goggle]] of gigglers. I can't tell you how! It's too screaming funny, rabbit it all! O but you must, you must really! By the holy well of Mulhuddart I swear I'd give my chance of going to heaven to hear it all, every word! O, leave me my faculties, woman, a while. If you don't like my story get out of the [[punt]]. Well, have it your own way, so. Here, sit down and do as you're bid. [[Lisp it slaney]] and [[crisp it]] quiet. Tell me [[longsome]]. Take your time now. Breathe deep. That's the [[fairway]]. Hurry [[slow]] and [[scheldt]] you go. Give us your [[blessed]] ashes here till I scrub the canon's underpants. [[Flow now. Ower more.]]

First she let her hair fall and down it [[flussed]] to her feet [[[its teviots winding coils]]]. Then, mothernaked, she washed herself with bogwater and mudsoap, upper and lower from crown to sole. Next she greased the groove of her keel with antifouling butterscotch [[[and turfentine [50] and serpenthyme]]] and with leafmould she [[ushered [51] round prunella]] isles and islets dun all over her little mary. And after that she wove a garland for her hair. She pleated it. She plaited it. Of meadowgrass and riverflags, the bulrush and waterweed, and of fallen leaves of weeping willow. Then she made her bracelets and her anklets and her armlets and a jetty amulet for necklace of clicking cobbles and pattering pebbles and rumbledown rubble, [[richmond and]] [52] rare, of Irish rhinestones and shellmarble bangles. That done, [[a dawk of smut to her airy ey, and]] she sent her [[boudeloire]] maid to His Affluence with [[respecks]] from his missus, seepy and sewery, and a request she might leave him for a [[minnikin]]. She said she wouldn't be [[half her]] length away. Then, then, with her mealiebag slung over her shoulder, Anna Livia, oysterface, out at last she came.

Describe her! Bustle along, why can't you? [[Spitz]] on the [[iern]] while it's hot. I wouldn't miss her for the world. I [[mussel]], I absolute must hear that! What had she on, the little old oddity? How much did she [[scallop]], harness and weights! Here she is. Amnisty Ann. Call her calamity electrifies man.

No electress at all, [[but old Moppa Necessity, mother of injins]]. I'll tell you now. But you must sit still. Will you hold your peace and listen well to what I am going to say now? It might have been ten

ANNA LIVIA PLURABELLE

or twenty to one when the [[flip]] of her [[hoogly]] igloo [[fluttered]] and out stepped a fairy woman, the dearest little mother ever you saw, nodding around her, all smiles, between two ages, a judyqueen, [[not up to]] your [[elb]]. And look at her sharp and seize her quick for the longer she lives the shorter she grows. [[Save us and tagus!]] No more? Why where did you ever [[[pick]]] a [[Lambay]] chop as big as a battering ram? Ay, you're right. I was forgetting. The height of [[my hough]], I say! She wore a ploughboy's nailstudded clogs, a pair of ploughfields in themselves: a sugarloaf hat with a [[gaudyquivery]] peak and a band of gorse and a hundred streamers dancing off it and a golden pin to pierce it: owlglassy bicycles boggled her eyes: and a fishnet veil she had to keep the sun from spoiling her wrinkles: potatorings buckled the loose ends of her ears: her nude cuba stockings were [[salmospotspeckled]]:[53] she sported a shimmy of hazegrey that once was blue till it ran in the washing: stout stays, the rivals, lined her length: her bloodorange knickers showed natural nigger boggers, fancy fastened, free to undo: her blackstripe tan joseph was teddybearlined, with wavy [[rushgreen]] epaulettes and a [[leadown]] here and there of [[royal swansruff]]: a brace of gaspers stuck in her hayrope garters: her civvy coat was boundaried round with a twobar tunnel belt: she had a clothespeg tight astride of her nose and she kept on grinding something quaint in her mouth and the tail of her snuffdrab shuiler's skirt trailed [[[fifty]]] [54] Irish miles behind her on the road.

Hellsbells, I'm sorry I missed her! [[Sweet umptyum and nobody fainted.]] But in [[whelk]] of her mouths? Was her [[naze]] alight? Everyone that saw her said the douce little [delia] looked a bit queer. [[Lotsy trotsy, mind the poddle!]] [55] Funny poor frump she must have [[charred]].[56] [[Kickhams]] a [[[rummier]]] ever you saw. [[Making saft [57] mullet's eyes at her boys dobelong.]] [And they crowned her the queen of the may. Of the may?] [[You don't say!]] Well for her she couldn't see herself. [I warrant that's why she murrayed [58] her mirror. She did? Mersey me!] There was a gang of drouthdropping surfacemen, boomslanging and plugchewing, lolling and leasing on Lazy Wall [[by the Jook of Yoick's]] [59] and as soon as they saw her [meander] by [in her grasswinter's weeds] and

TEXT D

twigged who was [under her deaconess bonnet, Avondale's] fish and [Clarence's] poison, says one to another: *Between me and you and the granite we're warming, as round as a hoop, Alp has doped.*

But what was the game in her mixed bag? I want to get it while it's fresh. I bet my beard it's worth while poaching on. Shake it up, do, do! I promise I'll make it worth your while. And I don't mean maybe. Tell me [[more but]] tell me true.

Well, [[arondgirond]] she pattered and swung and sidled, [dribbling her boulder through [60] narrows of mosses], not knowing which [medway] to [strike it] like Santa Claus at the call of the pale and puny with a Christmas box apiece for each and everyone of her childer. [The rivulets ran to see], [[the glashaboys, the pollynooties]]. And they all about her, youths and maidens, [rickets and riots], chipping her, and raising a bit of a jeer or cheer every time she'd dip in her [[culdee]] sack of rubbish she robbed and reach out her maundy merchandise, stinkers and heelers, laggards and primeboys, her [[furzeborn]] sons and [[dribbledary]] daughters, a thousand and one of them, and [[wickerpotluck]] for each of them. A tinker's [[bann]] and a [barrow] to boil his billy for Gipsy Lee: a cartridge of cockaleekine [61] soup for Tommy the Soldier: for sulky Pender's acid nephew deltoïd drops, curiously strong: a cough and a rattle and wildrose cheeks for poor little Petite [[MacFarlane]]: a jigsaw puzzle of needles and pins and blankets and shins between them for Isabel and Llewelyn Marriage: a brazen nose and pigiron mittens for Johnny Walker Beg: [[[a]]] [62] papal flag of the saints and stripes for Kevineen O'Dea: a puffpuff for Pudge Craig and a nightmarching hare for Toucher Doyle: waterleg and gumboots each for Bully Hayes and Hurricane Hartigan: a prodigal heart and fatted calves for Buck Jones, the pride of Clonliffe: a loaf of bread and a father's early kick for Tim from Skibereen: a jauntingcar for Larry Doolin, the Ballyclee jackeen: a seasick trip on a government ship for [[[Teague]]] O'Flanagan: a louse and trap for Jerry Coyle: [slushmincepies] for Andy MacKenzie: a hairclip and clackdish for Penceless Peter: a spellingbee book for Rosy Brooke; a drowned doll for Sister Anne [[Mortimer]]: [a snake in clover and a vaticanned vipercatcher's visa for Patsy Presbys]: scruboak beads for [beatified]

ANNA LIVIA PLURABELLE

Biddy: [[two appletweed stools]] [63] for Eva [[Mobbely]]: for Sara Philpot a jordan [vale] tearjar: a pretty box of pettyfib's powder for Eileen Alannah to whiten her teeth [and [[outflash]] [64] [[[Helen]]] [65] Arhone]: a whippingtop for Eddy Lawless: for Kitty Coleraine of Buttermilk Lane a penny wise for her foolish pitcher: a putty shovel for Larry the Puckaun: a potamus mask for Promoter Dunne: a dynamite egg for Paul the Curate: a [[tibertine's]] pile with a [Congoswood] cross on the back for Sunny Jim: [for Camilla, Dromilla, Ludmilla, Mamilla, a bucket, a packet, a book and a pillow]: for Nancy Shannon a Tuam brooch: for Dora Hopeandwater a cooling douche and a warmingpan: a pair of Blarney breeks for Wally Meagher: a hairpin slatepencil for Elsie Oram to scratch her toby, doing her best with her volgar fractions: an old age pension for Betty the Beauty: a bag of the blues for Funny Fitz: Jill, the spoon of a girl, for Jack, the broth of a boy: a [[Rogerson]] Crusoe Friday fast for [Caducus] Angelus [Rubiconstein]: three hundred and sixtysix poplin [[tyne]] for [[revery]] [warp] in the [weaver's] [[woof]] for Victor Hugonot: a rake and good [66] muck for Kate the Cleaner: a hole in the ballad for Hosty: two dozen of cradles for J.F.X.P. Coppinger: a letter to last a lifetime for Maggy beyond by the ashpit: the [heftiest frozenmeat] woman from Lusk to Livienbad for Felim the Ferry: spas and speranza for Gouty Gough: [a change of naves [67] and joys [68] of ills for Armoricus Tristram Amoor [69] Saint Lawrence]: [70] [[a C_3 peduncle for Karmalite Kane]]: a sunless map of the [month], including the [sword] and [stamps] for [Shemus O'Shaun] the Post: [a jackal [71] with hide for Browne but Nolan]: a stonecold shoulder for Donn Joe Vance: [[all]] lock and [[no]] stable for Honorbright Meretrix: a big drum for Billy Dunboyne: [72] whatever you like to [[swilly]] to drink, [Yuinness or Yennessy, Lagen or Niger], for Festus King and Roaring Peter and Frisky Shorty and Treacle Tom and [O.B.] Behan and Sully the Thug and Master Magrath and Peter Cloran and whoever you chance to meet knocking around: and a bladder balloon for Selina Susquehana Stakelum. But what did she give to Pruda Ward and Peggy Quilty and Nora Brosna and Teasy Kieran and Ena Lappin [[and Flora Ferns and Fauna Fox-Goodman]] and Una and Bina and Trina [[La Mesme]] and Philomena O'Farrell and [Irmak

TEXT D

Elly and] [73] Josephine Foyle and [[Snakeshead]] Lily and [[Fountainoy]] Laura and Mary Xavier Agnes Daisy Francis de Sales MacCabe? She gave them every mother's daughter a moonflower and a [bloodleaf]. [So on] Izzy, her [shamemaid], love [shone befond] her [tears [74] as from] Shem, her [penmight], life [past befoul] his [prime].

My colonial, what a bagful! That's what you may call a tale of a tub. [All that and more under one crinoline envelope if you dare to break the [[porkbarrel]] seal.] No wonder they'd run from her like the plague. Throw us [your hudson] soap for the honour of [Clane]. The wee [[taste]] the water left. You've all the swirls your side of the current. Well, am I to blame for that if I have? Who said you're to blame for that if you have? My hands are as blue between cold and soda as that piece of pattern chayney there, lying below. Or where is it? Lying beside the reeds I saw it. [Hoangho, my sorrow, I've lost it!] With that peaty water who could see? But O, go on. I love a gabber. I could listen to more and [maure] again. Rain [onder] river. Flies [do] your float. [Thick] is the life for [mere].

Well, you know or don't you know or haven't I told you every story has an end [[and that's the he and the she of it]]. Look, look, the dusk is growing. What time is it? It must be late. It's ages now since I or anyone last saw Waterhouse's clock. They took it asunder, I heard them say. When will they reassemble it? O, my back, my back, my back! [[I'd want to go to Aches-les-Pains.]] [75] Wring out the clothes! Wring in the dew! Will we spread them here now? Ay, we will. Spread on your bank and I'll spread mine on mine. It's what I'm doing. Spread! It's [[churning]] chill. [[Der went]] [76] is rising. I'll lay a few stones on the hotel sheets. A man and his bride embraced between them. Else I'd have sprinkled and folded them only. And I'll tie my butcher's apron here. It's suety yet. The strollers will pass it by. Six shifts, ten kerchiefs, the convent [77] napkins twelve, one baby's shawl. Where are all her childer now? Some here, more no more, more again lost to the stranger I've heard tell that same brooch of the Shannons was married into a family in Spain. And all the Dunnes beyond Brendan's sea takes number nine in hats. And one of Biddy's beads went bobbing till she rounded up last [[hister-

ANNA LIVIA PLURABELLE

eve]] with a marigold and a cobbler's candle in a main drain off Bachelor's Walk. But all that's left to the last of the Meaghers [78] is one kneebuckle and two hooks in the front. Do you tell me that now? I do, in troth. [Oronoko! What's the trouble?] Is that the great [[Finnleader]] himself [[in his joakimono]] [79] on his statue riding [[the]] high horse there [[forehengist]]? There? Is it that? On Fallareen Common? Throw the cobwebs from your eyes, woman, and spread your washing proper. It's well I know your sort of slop. Were you lifting your elbow, tell us, glazy cheeks, in the Carrigacurra canteen? Was I what, [[hobbledyhips]]? Amn't I up since the damp dawn with varicose veins, soaking and bleaching boiler rags, and sweating cold, a widow like me, to deck my tennis champion son, the laundryman with the lavender [80] flannels? Holy [[Scamander]]! [81] I saw it again! Near the golden falls. [[Icis on us!]] There! Subdue your noise, you poor creature! What is it but a blackberry growth or the [[dwyergray]] ass them four old codgers owns. Are you [[maining]] Tarpey and Lyons and Gregory? I mean [now] [[thank all]], [the] four [of them and the roar of them that] owns that stray in the mist and old Johnny MacDougal along with them. Is that the Poolbeg flasher [beyant] or the mast of a coaster [nigh] the Kish or a glow I behold within a hedge? Wait till the rising of the moon. My [sights are swimming] thicker on me [by] the shadows [to] this place. I'll [[sow]] [82] home slowly now [by] own way, [[moyvalley]] [83] way. [[Row]] will I too, [[rathmine]].[84]

Ah, but she was the queer old skeowsha anyhow, Anna Livia, twinkletoes And sure he was the queer old buntz too, Dear Dirty Dumpling, foostherfather of [fingalls and] [[dotthergills]].[85] Gammer and gaffer we're all their gangsters.[86] Hadn't he seven dams to wive him? And every dam had her seven crutches. And every crutch had its seven hues. And each hue had a [differing] cry. Suds for me and supper for you and the doctor's bill for John Joe. Before! Before! He married his markets, cheap by foul, I know, but at [[milkidmass]] who was the spouse? Then all that was was fair. [In elvenland?] [87] Teems of times and happy returns. The same anew. [[Ordovico or viricordo.]] [88] [Anna was, Livia is, Plurabelle's to be. Northmen's thing made southfolk's place but howmulty [[plurators]] [89] made

TEXT D

eachone in person? Latin me that, my trinity scholard. *Hircus Civis Eblanensis*!] He had buckgoat paps on him, soft ones for orphans. Ho, Lord! Twins of his bosom. Lord save us. And ho! Hey? What all men. Hot? His tittering daughters of. Whawk?

Can't hear with the waters of. The chittering waters of. Flittering bats, fieldmice bawk talk. Ho! Are you not gone ahome? What Tom Malone? Can't hear with bawk of bats, all the liffeying waters of. Ho, talk save us! My foos [[won't]] [90] moos. I feel as old [91] as yonder elm. A tale told of Shaun or Shem? All, Livia's daughtersons. Dark hawks hear us! Night! Night! My ho head halls. I feel as heavy as yonder stone. Tell me of John or Shaun? Who were Shem and Shaun the living sons or daughters of? Night now! Tell me, tell me, tell me, elm! Night night! Tell me tale of stem or stone. Beside the rivering waters of, hitherandthithering waters of. Night!

꜀ ꜀ ꜀ ꜀ ꜀ TEXT E

O TELL me all about Anna Livia![1] I want to hear all about Anna Livia. Well, you know Anna Livia? Yes, of course, we all know Anna Livia. Tell me all. Tell me now. You'll die when you hear. Well, you know, when the old [[[cheb]]] went futt and did what you know. Yes, I know, go on. Wash away and don't be dabbling. Tuck up your sleeves and loosen your talk-tapes. Or whatever it was they try to make out he tried to do in the Fiendish park. He's an awful old rep. Look at the shirt of him! Look at the dirt of it! He has all my water black on me. And it steeping and stuping since this time last [wek].[2] How many [[[goes]]] is it I wonder he washed it? I know by heart the places he likes to [[[saale, duddurty devil]]]! Scorching my hand and starving my famine to make his private linen public. Wallop it well with your battle and clean it. My wrists are rusty rubbing the mouldaw stains. And the dneepers of wet and the gangres of sin in it! What was it he did [a tail][3] at all on Animal [[Sendai]]? And how long was he under lough and neagh? It was put in the papers what he did, [nicies and priers, the King fierceas Humphrey, with] illysus distilling, [[exploits]] and all. But [[[toms]]] will tell. I know [[[he]]] will. [[[Temp]]] [[untamed]] will [[hist]] for no man. O, the [[[roughty]]] old rep! And the cut of him! And the strut of him! How he used to hold his head as high as a howeth, the famous [[[eld]]] duke alien, with a hump of grandeur on him like a walking rat. [And his derry's own drawl and

NOTE: This text is a composite of the *Navire* text, the *transition* proofs, and the Yale copy for the Gaige galleys. Emendations between the *Calendar* galleys and the *transition* galleys are enclosed in single brackets; emendations which occur also in the *Navire* text are noted. Emendations on the *transition* galleys are enclosed in double brackets. Emendations on the two sets of page proof and the Yale copy are enclosed in triple brackets.

60

TEXT E

his corksown blather and his doubling stutter and his gullaway swank. Ask Lictor Hackett or Lector Reade or Garda Growley or the Boy with the Billyclub.] [[How]] [[[elster]]] [4] is he [[a called]] at all. [[[Qu'appelle?]]] [Huges Caput Earlyfouler?] Or where was he born or how was he found? [[Urgothland, Tvistown, on the Kattekat? New Hunshire, Concord, on the Merrimake?]] [5] [Was her banns never loosened in Adam and Eve's] and were him and her ever spliced [Flowey and Mount on the brink of time [[makes]] [6] wishes and fears for a happy isthmass? O, [[[passmore]]] [7] that and oxus another! Don Dom Domb domb and his wee follyo!] I heard he dug good tin with his doll when he [[raped]] her home, [[Sabrine]] asthore, in a parakeet's cage, [by dredgerous lands and devious delts, playing catched and mythed with the gleam of her shadda], [[past auld min's manse, and Maisons Allfou and the rest of incurables and the last of immurables]], the quaggy [[[waag]]] for stumbling. Who sold you that jackalantern's tale? In a gabbard he [[barqued it]], the boat of life, [from the harbourless Ivernikan Okean], [[till he [8] spied the loom of his landfall]] and he loosed two croakers from under his tilt, the [[[gran]]] Phenician rover. By the smell of her kelp they made the pigeonhouse. Like fun they did! But where was Himself, [[the timoneer]]? That marchantman he follied their scutties right over the wash, his cameleer's burnous breezing up on him, till with his runagate bowmpriss he [[roade]] and borst her bar. [[Pilcomayo! Suchcaughtawan!]] [9] [And the whale's away with the grayling!] Tune your pipes and fall ahumming, you born ijypt, and you're nothing short of one! [Well, ptellomey soon and curb your froth.] When they saw him shoot swift up her sheba sheath, like any gay lord salomon, her bulls they were [[ruhring]], surfed with spree. [[[Boyarka buah! Boyana bueh!]]] He erned his lille Bunbath hard, our staly bread, the trader. He did. Look at here. In this wet of his prow. Don't you know he was [[[kalled]]] a bairn of the [[[brine]]], [[Wasserbourne]] the waterbaby? [[Havemmarea]], so he was. H.C.E. has a [[[codfish]]] ee. [[[Shyr]]], she's nearly as [[[badher]]] as him herself. Who? Anna Livia? Ay, Anna Livia. Do you know she was calling backwater [[[sals]]] from all around to go in till him, her erring man, and tickle the pontiff [[aisy-

ANNA LIVIA PLURABELLE

oisy]]?[10] She was? [[Gota]] pot! [[Well, that's the limmat! As El Negro said when he looked in La Plate.]] O, tell me all I want to hear. Letting on she didn't care, the proxenete! Proxenete and phwhat[11] is phthat? [Tell us in franca langua.] Did they never [[sharee]] you ebro at skol, [[you anti-abecedarian]]?[12] It's just the same as if I was to go for [[examplum]] now [out of telekinesis] and proxenete you. For [[coxyt']] sake and is that what she is? [[[Botlettle]]][13] [I thought she'd act that] [[[loa]]].[14] Didn't you spot her in her [[[windaug]]], wubbling up on an osiery chair, [with a [[meusic]][15] before her all cunniform letters], pretending to ribble a reedy derg on a fiddle she [[[bogans]]] without a [[band on]]? Sure she can't fiddan a dee, [[with]] bow or [[abandon]]! Srue, she can't! [[[Tista]]] suck. Well, I never heard the like of that! Tell me more. Tell me most. Well, old Humber was as [[glommen]] as grampus, [[with the tares at his thor and the buboes[16] for ages and neither bowman nor shot abroad, and bales ablaze on[17] the crests[18] of rockies[19] and [[[nera]]][20] lamp in kitchen or church and giant's holes in Grafton's causeway]], setting [[[sambre]]] on his benk, [[drammen and drummm,[21] his childlinen scarf to encourage his obsequies]], where he'd check their debths in that mormon's thames, hungerstriking all alone and holding doomsdag over [[[hunseself]]], dreeing his weird, with his dander up, and his fringe combed over his eygs and [[[droming]]][22] on loft till the sight of the sternes, [after [[zwarthy]][23] kowse and weedy broeks[24] and the tits of buddy and the loits of pest and to peer was Parish worth [[thette]][25] mess]. You'd think all was [[[dodo]]] belonging to him [[how[26] he [[[durmed adranse]]][27] in durance vaal]]. He had been belching for severn years. And there she was, Anna Livia, she darent catch a winkle of sleep, purling around like a chit of a child, in a Lapsummer skirt and damazon cheeks, [for to [[[ishim]]][28] bonzour to her dear dubber Dan].[29] [[With neuphraties and sault[30] from his maggias.]] And an odd time she'd cook him up blooms of fisk and lay to his heartsfoot her meddery eygs and staynish beacons on toasc and a cupenhave [so weeshywashy] of Greenland's tay [[or [[[a dzoupgan of kaffue]]] mokau[31] to order or Si-kiang]] [[[sukry]]] [or his ale of ferns in trueart pewter] and a [[[shinkobread]]] for to plaise that

TEXT E

man hog stay his stomicker [32] till her pyrraknees shrunk to nutmeg graters and as rash as she'd [[[russ]]] with her peakload of vivers up on her [[[sieve]]] [(his towering rage see how it [[swales and]] rises!)] my [[[hardey]]] Hek he'd kast them [[[frome]]] him, with a stour of scorn, as much as to say you [[[sow]]] and you [[[sozh]]], and if he didn't peg the [[platteau on]] her [[[tawe]]],[33] believe [you] me, she was safe enough. And then she'd [[esk]] to vistule a hymn, *The Heart Bowed Down* or *The Rakes of Mallow* [[or Chelli Michele's *La Calumnia è un Vermicelli* or a balfy bit or *old Jo Robidson*]]. [[[Sucho]]] [34] [fuffing] [[[a]]] [35] [fifeing] [[twould cut you in two]]! [She'd bate the hen that crowed on the turrace of Babbel.] What harm if she knew how to cockle her mouth. And not a mag out of Hum no more than out of the mangle weight. Is that a faith? That's a fact. [Then doing the ricka and [[[roya romanche]]],[36] Annona, gebroren [[[aroostokrat]]] Nivia, [[with Sparks' pirryphlickathims funkling her fan]], her [[[frostivied]]] [37] tresses [[[dasht]]] [38] with [[[virevlies]]],[39] [[— while the prom beauties sreeked [40] in their bearers' skins!—]] in a period gown of changeable jade that would [[[robe]]] [41] the woost of two cardinals' chairs and crush poor Cullen and smother Mac Cabe.] And brahming to him down the feedchute, with all kinds of fondling endings, the poother rambling off her nose: *Vuggybarney, Wickerymandy! Hello, ducky, please don't die!* Do you know what she started cheeping then, the voice of her like a watergluck? You'll never guess. Tell me. Tell me. *Phoebe, dearest, tell, O tell me* and *I loved you better nor you knew.* And letting on she was daft about the warbly sangs from over holmen: *High hellskirt saw ladies hensmoker lilyhung pigger*: [[[and soay and sohan in a tone sonora]]] and Oom Bothar below in his sandy cloak, [[[so umvolosy]]], as deaf as a yawn. Go away! [Poor deef, old] [[[deary]]]! [42] [[Yare]] only [[teesing]]! Anna Liv? As chalk is my judge! And didn't she up and rise and go and trot [[[doon]]] and stand in [her douro], puffing her old dudheen, and every [[[shirvant siligirl]]] or [[[wensum]]] farmerette walking the pilend roads [Sawy, Fundally, Daery or Maery, Milucre, Awny or Graw], usedn't she make her a [[[simp or]]] sign to slip inside by the sullyport? You don't say the sillypost? I did. And do. Calling

ANNA LIVIA PLURABELLE

them in one by one [[(To Blockbeddum! [43] here! Here the Shoebenacaddie!)]] and legging a jig or so [[on the sihl]] to show them how to shake their benders and the dainty how to bring to mind the gladdest garments out of sight and all the way of a maid with a man and making a sort of a cackling noise like two and a penny or half a crown and holding up a [[[silliver]]] shiner. Lordy, lordy, did she so? Well, of all the ones ever I heard! Throwing all the [[[neiss]]] [44] [[little whores in]] the world at him! To [[[inny]]] [captured] [[wench]] you [[wish]] of no matter what sex of [[[pleissful]]] ways two [[[adda]]] [45] [[tammar a lizzy a]] [[[lossie]]] [46] to hug and [[[hab]]] [haven] in Humpy's apron!

And what was the wyerye [[[rima]]] she made! O that! Tell me [[the trent of it]] while I'm [47] lathering [[[hail]]] out of Denis Florence MacCarthy's combies. I'm dying down off my iodine feet until I hear Anna Livia's cushingloo! I can see that, I see you are. How does it [[tummel]]? Listen now. Are you listening? Yes, yes! [Idneed] [48] I am! [[Tarn your [[[ore]]] [49] ouse.[50] Essonne inne.]]

By earth and [the cloudy] but I badly want a brandnew bankside, bedamp and I do, and a plumper at that!

For the putty affair I have is wore out, so it is, sitting, yaping and waiting for my old Dane the dodderer, my life in death companion, my frugal key of our larder, my muchaltered camel's hump, my jointspoiler, my maymoon's honey, my fool to the last Decemberer, to wake himself out of his winter's doze and [[bore]] me down like he used to.

Is there [[irwell]] a lord of the manor or a knight of the shire at all, I wonder, that'd [dip] [51] me a pound or two in cash for washing and darning his worshipful socks for him now we're run out of horsemeat and milk?

Only for my short Brittas bed [made] is as snug as it smells it's out I'd lep and offwith me to the slobs of the Tolka or the shores of Clontarf to [[[feale]]] the gay [[aire]] of my salttroublin bay and the race of the saywint up me ambushure.

[[[Onon! Onon! Tel]]] me more. Tell [52] me every tiny [[[teign]]]. I want to know every single [[[ingul]]]. [[[Down to what made the potters fly into jagsthole. And why were the vesles vet.]]] Well, now

TEXT E

comes the hazelhatchery part. [[After Clondalkin the Kings's Inns. We'll soon be there with the freshet.]] How many aleveens had she in [tool]?⁵³ I can't rightly tell you that. Close only knows. Some say she had [three figures to fill and confined herself to] a hundred eleven.⁵⁴ She can't remember half the cradlenames she smacked on them by the grace of her boxing bishop's infallible slipper. A hundred and how? They did well to [[rechristien]]⁵⁵ her Plurabelle. O loreley! What a [[[loddon]]] [loads]! She must have been a [gadabout]⁵⁶ in her day, so she must, more than most. Shoal she was, [[[gidgad]]].⁵⁷ She had a flewmen of her owen. Tell me, tell me, how [[[cam]]] she [[[camlin]]] through all her fellows, [the neckar she was], the [[diveline]]? Linking one and knocking the next, [[[tapting]]]⁵⁸ [[a flank and [[[tipting]]]⁵⁹ a jutty]]⁶⁰ and palling in and [[[pietaring]]] out and clyding by on her eastway. [[Waiwhou]] was the first [[[thurever]]] burst? Someone [he] was, [[[whuebra]]] [they were], [[in a tactic attack or in single combat]]. Tinker, [[[tilar, souldrer]]], [[salor]], [[[Pieman Peace]]] or [[[Polistaman]]].⁶¹ That's the thing I always want to know. [Push up and push upper and come to headquarters! Was it [[waterlows]]⁶² year, after Grattan or Flood, or when maids were in Arc or when three stood hosting? [[[Fidaris]]]⁶³ will find where the Doubt arises like [[[Niemen]]]⁶⁴ from Nirgends found the Nihil. Worry you sighin foh, Albern, O Anser? Untie the gemman's fistiknots, Qwic and Nuancee?] She can't put her hand on him for the moment. [[[Tez thelon langlo]]], walking weary! Such a [[[loon]]] way backwards to row! She says herself she hardly knows [[whuon⁶⁵ the annals]] her graveller was, [[a dynast of Leinster, a wolf of the sea]], or what he did or how [[[blyth]]] she played or when and where and how often he [[jumnped]] her. She was just a young thin pale soft shy slim slip of a thing then, sauntering, and he was a heavy trudging lurching lieabroad of a Curraghman, making his hay for the sun to shine on, as tough as the oaktrees (peats be with them!) used to rustle that time down by the dykes of killing Kildare, that forstfellfoss with a plash across her. She thought she'd [[[sankh neathe]]] the ground with [[nymphant]]⁶⁶ shame when he gave her the tigris eye! [[O happy fault! Me wish it was he!]] You're wrong there, corribly

ANNA LIVIA PLURABELLE

wrong! [[Tisn't only tonight you're anacheronistic!]] It was ages behind that when nullahs were nowhere, in county Wickenlow, garden of Erin, before she ever dreamt she'd [[lave]] Kilbride and go [[foaming]] under Horsepass bridge [[with the great southerwestern windstorming her traces and the midlands' grainwaster [67] asarch for her track]], to wend her ways byandby, rebecca or worse, [[to spin and to grind, to swab and to thrash]],[68] in the barleyfields and pennylotts of Humphrey's fordofhurdlestown and lie with a landleaper, wellingtonorseher. [[Alas [69] the lakes of girly days! For the dove of the dunas!]] Wasut? Izod? Are you [[sarthe and]] [70] suir? [Not where the Finn fits into the Mourne, not where the Nore takes lieve of Blœm, not where the [[[Braye]]] [71] divarts the Farer, not where the Moy [[[changez]]] [72] her [[minds]] [73] [[[twixt]]] [74] Cullin and Conn] [[[tween Cunn and Collin]]]? [75] [[Neya, narev]], [[[nen]]] [and] [[[nos]]]! [76] [Then] whereabouts in Ow and Ovoca? Was it [[[ystwith [77] wyst]]] or Lucan Yokan or where the hand of man has never set foot? [[Dell]] me where, the very [[[ferse]]] time! I will if you listen. You know the [[[dinkel]]] [78] [[dale]] of Luggelaw? Well, there once dwelt a local heremite, Michael Arklow was his [riverend] [79] name, (with many a sigh I aspersed his lavabibs!) and one venersderg in junojuly [[[oso]]] sweet and so [[[cool]]] and so limber she looked, [Nance the Nixie, Nanon L'Escaut, in the silence, of the sycomores, all listening],[80] the kind of curves you simply can't stop feeling, he plunged both of his [[newly]] anointed hands up to [[[his cushlas]]] [81] in her [[[singimari]]] saffron [[[strumans]]] of hair, parting them and soothing her and mingling it, that was [deepdark] [82] and ample like the red bog at sundown. [[Maass!]] He [cuddle not] [83] help himself, [[[thurso that]]] hot on him, he had to forget the monk in the man so, rubbing her up and smoothing her down, he [[[baised]]] his [[[lippes]]] in smiling mood, kiss [[akiss]] after [[[kisokushk]]] [84] (as he warned her never to, never to, never) on [Annana-Poghue's of the] [85] freckled forehead. [[[While you'd parse [86] secheressa she hielt her souf.]]] O, wasn't he the bold priest? And wasn't she the naughty Livvy? [[Nautic]] [87] [Naama's] [88] [[now]] her [navn]. Two lads in their breeches went through her before that, Barefoot Burn and [[Wary]] Wade, Lugnaquillia's noble pair, before

TEXT E

she had a hint of a hair at her fanny to hide [[or a bossom to tempt a birch canoedler [89] not to mention a bulgy porterhorse barge]]. And ere that again, [[ledy, ledy, all unredy, too faint to buoy the fairiest rider, too frail to flirt with a cygnet's plume]], she was licked by a hound [[Chirripa]]-[[[Chirruta]]],[90] while poing her pee, pure and simple, on the spur of the hill in old Kippure, in birdsong and shearingtime, but first of all, worst of all, [the wiggly livvly], she sideslipped out by a gap in the Devil's glen while Sally her nurse was sound asleep in a sloot and fell over a spillway before she found her stride and lay and wriggled in all the stagnant black pools of [[[rainy]]] under a fallow [coo] and she laughed innocefree with her limbs aloft and a whole drove of maiden hawthorns blushing and looking askance upon her.

Drop me the sound of the [[[findhorn's]]] [91] name. And drip me why in the [[[flenders]]] [92] was she [[[frickled]]]. And trickle me through was she [[marcellewaved]] or was it weirdly a wig she wore. [And whitside did they droop their glows in their florry, aback to wist or affront to sea?] [[In fear to hear the dear so near or [93] longing loth and loathing longing?]] Are you in the swim or are you out? O go on, go on, go on! I mean about what you know. I know right well what you mean. [[[You'd like the coifs and guimpes, snouty, and me to do the greasy jub on old Veronica's wiper.]]] What am I [[[rancing]]] now and I'll thank you? Is it a pinny or is it a surplice? Arran, where's your nose? And where's the starch? That's not the [[[vesdre]]] benediction smell. I can tell from here by their *eau de* [*Colo*] and the scent of her [[oder]] they're Mrs. Magrath's. And you ought to have [[[aird]]] them. They've [[moist]] come off her. Creases in silk they are, not crampton lawn. [[[Baptiste me, father, for she has sinned!]]] [Through her catchment ring she freed them easy, with her hips'hurrahs for her knees'dontelleries.] The only [[[paar]]] with frills in old the plain. So they are. [[[Welland]]] well! And [[[here]]] [94] is her nubilee letters too. Ellis on quay in scarlet thread. [Linked for the world on a flushcoloured field.] [[Annan exe]] after to show they're not Laura Kehoe's. O, may the [[diabolo]] [twisk] your [[seifety]] pin! [You child of Mammon, Kinsella's Lilith!] Now who has been tearing the leg of her drawers on her? Which

ANNA LIVIA PLURABELLE

leg is it? The one with the bells on it. Rinse them out and aston along with you. Where did I stop? Never stop. Continuarration. You're not there yet. Garonne, garonne!

Well, after it was put in the Beggars' [[[Sitterdag-Zindeh-Munaday Wakeschrift]]] [95] [(for once they sullied their white kid gloves with their show us it here and, their mind out of that and their when youre quite finished with the reading] [[matarial]]),[96] even the [snee] that [snowdon] his hoaring hair had a skunner against him. [[Thaw, thaw, sava, savuto!]] Everywhere [[[erriff]]] you went and every bung you [[[arver]]] dropped into, [in cit or [[[subur]]] [97] or in added areas], [[the Rose and Bottle or Phoenix Tavern or Power's Inn or Jude's Hotel]], or wherever you scoured the countryside from Nannywater to Vartryville, [[or from Porta Lateen to the lootin quarter]] you found his [[[ikom]]] [[etsched tipside]] [98] down or the cornerboys burning his guy and [[Morris]] the Man, [[with the role of a royss in his turgos the turrible, Evropeahahn cheic house, unskimmed sooit and yahoort, hammam now cheekmee, Ahdahm this way make, Fatima, half turn]], reeling and [[railing]] around the local with oddfellow's triple tiara busby rotundarinking round his scalp. [Like Pate-by-the-Neva or Pete-over-Meer. This is the Hausman all paven and stoned, that cribbed the Cabin that never was owned, that cocked his leg and hennad his Egg. And the [[mauldrin]] rabble around him in areopage making a great fracas [[[bingkang]]] [99] with their [[timpan]] crowders. Mind, your Grimmfather. Think of your Ma!] She swore [[on croststyx]] she'd be level with all [[the snags]] of them yet. [[Par [100] the [101] Vulnerable Virgins' Mary del Dam!]] [102] So she said to herself she'd frame a plan to fake a shine, the mischiefmaker, the like of it you [[[niever]]] heard. What plan? Tell me [[quick and [[[dongu]]] [103] so crould]]! What the [[[meurther]]] did she [[[mague]]]? Well, she bergened a bag, a shammy mailbag, off one of her swapsons, Shaun the Post, and then she went [and consulted her [[[chapboucqs]]],[104] old [[Mot]] Moore, Casey's Euclid, and the Fashion Display] and made herself [[tidal to join in [105] the mascarete]]. O goggle of [[[gigguels]]], I can't tell you how! It's too screaming funny, rabbit it all! O but you must, you must really! By the holy well of Mulhuddart I swear I'd [[pledge]] [106] my [[[chanza]]]

TEXT E

[getting] to heaven to hear it all, every word. O, leave me my faculties, woman, a while. If you don't like my story get out of the punt. Well, have it your own way, so. Here, sit down and do as you're bid. Lisp it slaney and crisp it quiet. [[[Deel]]] me longsome. [[[Tongue]]] your time now. Breathe [[[thet]]] deep. [[[Thouat's]]] the fairway. Hurry slow and scheldt you go. [[[Lynd]]] us your blessed ashes here till I scrub the canon's underpants. Flow now. Ower more.

First she let her hair fall and down it flussed to her feet its teviots winding coils. Then, mothernaked, she [[sampood]] herself with [[galawater]] and [[[fraguant mud, wupper and lauar]]], from crown to sole. Next she greased the groove of her keel, [[warthes and wears and mole and itcher]], with antifouling butterscotch and turfentine and serpenthyme and with leafmould she ushered round prunella isles and islets dun all over her little mary. And after that she wove a garland for her hair. She pleated it. She plaited it. Of meadowgrass and riverflags, the bulrush and waterweed, and of fallen [griefs] [107] of weeping willow. Then she made her bracelets and her anklets and her armlets and a jetty amulet for necklace of clicking cobbles and pattering pebbles and rumbledown rubble, richmond and [[[rehr]]], of Irish rhinestones and shellmarble bangles. That done, a dawk of smut to her airy ey [[and the lellipos cream to her lippeleens [108] and the pick of the paintbox for her pommettes, from strawberry reds to extray violates]],[109] and she sent her boudeloire [maids] to His Affluence-[Ciliegia] [[Grande]] [and Kirschie Real], [[[the two chirrines]]], with respecks from his missus, seepy and sewery, and a request she might leave him for minnikin. [A call to pay, and light a taper, in [[[Brie-on-Arrosa]]],[110] back in a] [[sprizzling]],[111] [[The cock striking mine, the stalls bridely sign, there's Zambosy waiting for me.]] She said [112] she wouldn't be half her length away. Then, then, [as soon as the lump his back was turned], with her mealiebag [[[slang]]] over her shoulder, Anna Livia, oysterface, [[[forth]]] [[of her]] [[[bassein]]] [113] came.

Describe her! [Hustle] [114] along, why can't you? Spitz on the iern while it's hot. I wouldn't miss her for [[[irthing in]]] the world. [[Oceans of God]], I mussel hear that! [[Ishekarry [115] and]] [[[washemeskad,[116] the carishy caratimaney]]]? What had she on, the [[[lid-

ANNA LIVIA PLURABELLE

del]]] old oddity! How much did she scallop, harness and weights! Here she is. Amnisty Ann. Call her calamity electrifies man.

No electress at all, but old Moppa Necessity, mother of injins. I'll tell you now. But you must sit still. Will you hold your peace and listen well to what I am going to say now? It might have been ten or twenty to one [of the night of All close or the nexth of April] when the flip of her hoogly igloo [[[flappered]]] and out stepped a fairy woman, the dearest little [[[moma]]] ever you saw, nodding around her, all smiles, [[with ems of embarras and aùes to awe]], between two ages, a judyqueen, not up to your elb. And look at her sharp and seize her [[[quirk]]] [117] for the [bicker] she lives the [slicker] she grows. Save us and tagus! No more? [[[Werra]]] where [[in [118] ourthe]] did you ever pick a Lambay chop as big as a battering ram? Ay, you're right. [[I'm epte to]] forgetting, [Like Liviam Liddle did Loveme Long]. The [[[linth]]] of my hough, I say! She wore a ploughboy's nailstudded clogs, a pair of ploughfields in themselves: a sugarloaf hat with a [[gaudyquiviry]] peak and a band of gorse [[for an arnoment]] and a hundred streamers dancing off it and a golden pin to pierce it: owlglassy bicycles boggled her eyes: and a [[fishnetzeveil]] she had to keep the sun from spoiling her wrinkles: potatorings [[boucled]] the loose [[[laubes]]] [119] of her [[[laudesnarers]]]:[120] her nude cuba stockings were salmospotspeckled: she sported a [[[galligo]]] shimmy of [[[hazevaipar]]] [[[tinto]]] that [[never]] was [[fast]] till it ran in the washing: stout stays, the rivals, lined her length: her bloodorange [[bockknickers, a two in one garment]], showed natural nigger boggers, fancyfastened, free to undo: her blackstripe tan joseph was [sequansewn and] teddybearlined, with wavy rushgreen epaulettes and a leadown here and there of royal swansruff: a brace of gaspers stuck in her hayrope garters: her civvy [[codroy]] coat [[with alpheubett buttons]] was boundaried round with a twobar tunnel belt: [[a fourpenny bit in [121] each pocketside [122] weighed her safe from the blowaway windrush]]; [123] she had a clothespeg tight astride of her [joki's] nose and she [kep] on grinding [[a sommething]] quaint in her [[fiumy]] [124] mouth and the [[rrreke of the]] [fluve of the] tail [of the gawan] of her snuffdrab

TEXT E

[[[siouler's]]] [125] skirt trailed [ffiffty] Irish miles behind her [[[lungarhodes]]].[126]

Hellsbells, I'm sorry I missed her! Sweet [[[gumptyum]]] and nobody fainted. But in whelk of her mouths? Was her naze alight? Everyone that saw her said the [[[dowce]]] [127] little delia looked a bit queer. Lotsy trotsy, mind the poddle! [Missus, be good and don't fol in the say!] [[[Fenny]]] poor [[[hex]]] she must have charred. Kickhams a [[[frumpier]]] ever you saw. Making saft mullet's eyes at her boys dobelong. And they crowned her the [[[chariton]]] queen of the may. Of the may? You don't say! Well for her she couldn't see herself. I [[[recknitz]]] that's why [[the darling]] murrayed her mirror. She did? Mersey me! There was a [[koros]] of drouthdropping surfacemen, boomslanging and plugchewing, [[[fruiteyeing]]] [128] [and flowerfeeding], [[in contemplation of the fluctuation and the undification of her filimentation]], lolling and leasing on Lazy [[[Waal]]] by the [[[Jukar]]] Yoick's and as soon as they saw her meander by in her grasswinter's weeds and twigged who was under her deaconess bonnet, Avondale's fish and Clarence's poison, says [[[an]]] to [[[anaber]]],[129] [Wit-upon-Crutches to Master Bates]: *Between me and you and the granite we're warming, as round as a hoop, Alp has doped.*

But what was the game in her mixed [[[baggyrhatty]]]? [[And where in thunder did she plunder? Fore the battle or efter the ball?]] I want to get it [frisk from the soorce]. I [[aubette]] my beard it's worth while poaching on. Shake it up, do, do! [That's a good old son of a ditch!] [130] I promise. I'll make it worth [131] your while. And I don't mean maybe. [[Spey]] me [[pruth and I'll tale you]] true.

Well, arondgirond [in a waveney] [[[lyne]]] [132] [[aringarouma]] she pattered and swung and sidled, dribbling her boulder through [[[narrowa]]] mosses, [the diliskydrear on our drier side and the vilde vetchvine agin us, [[[curara]]] [133] here careero there], not knowing which [134] medway [[or wheser]] [135] to strike it, [[[edereider]]], [[making chattahoochee all to her]] [136] [[[ain chichiu]]], like Santa Claus at the [[[cree]]] [137] of the pale and puny, [[[nistling]]] [138] [to hear for their tiny hearties], [[her arms encircling Isolabella, then running with reconciled Romus and Remes, then [139] bathing Dirty

ANNA LIVIA PLURABELLE

Hans'[140] spatters with spittle]], with a Christmas box apiece for [[[aisch]]] and [[[iveryone]]] of her childer, [[the birthday gifts they dreamt they [[[gabe]]] [141] her]]. The rivulets ran to see, the glashaboys, the pollynooties. [[Out of the paunshaup on to the pyre.]] And they all about her, youths and maidens, rickets and riots, [like the Smyly boys at their vicereine's levee], [[[vivi vienne]]],[142] [[little Anne, old Anna, high life]], [[[sing us a sula, O Susuria! hasn't she tambre?]]] chipping her and raising a bit of a [[[chir or a jary]]] every time she'd [neb] [143] in her culdee [[[sacco]]] of [[[wabbash]]] she [[[raabed]]] and reach out her maundy merchandise, stinkers and heelers, laggards and [primelads], her furzeborn sons and [dribblederry] [144] daughters, a thousand and one of them, and wickerpotluck for each of them. [For evil and ever. And kiks the buch.] A tinker's bann and a barrow to boil his billy for Gipsy Lee: a cartridge of cockaleekie [145] soup for [[[Chummy]]] the [[[Guardsman]]]: for sulky Pender's acid nephew deltoïd drops, curiously strong: a cough and a rattle and wildrose cheeks for poor little petite MacFarlane: a jigsaw puzzle of needles and pins and blankets and shins between them for Isabel, [[[Jezebel]]] [146] and Llewelyn Marriage: a brazen nose and pigiron mittens for Johnny Walker Beg: a papal flag of the saints and stripes for Kevineen O'Dea: a puffpuff for Pudge Craig and a nightmarching hare for [[[Techer Tombigby]]]:[147] waterleg and gumboots each for Bully Hayes and Hurricane Hartigan: a prodigal heart and fatted calves for Buck Jones, the pride of Clonliffe: a loaf of bread and a father's early [[aim]] for Tim from Skibereen: a jauntingcar for Larry Doolin, the Ballyclee jackeen: a seasick trip on a government ship for Teague O'Flanagan: a louse and trap for Jerry Coyle: slushmincepies for Andy Mackenzie: a hairclip and clackdish for Penceless Peter; [[that twelve sounds look]] for [[G. V.]] Brooke; a drowned doll for Sister Anne Mortimer: [[altar falls for Blanchisse's [148] bed; Wildairs' [[[breekies]]] [149] for Magpeg Woffington; [[[to]]] [150] Sue Dot a big eye [[[to]]] [151] Sam Dash a false step]]; a snake in clover and a vaticanned vipercatcher's visa for Patsy Presbys: [[a rise every [152] [[[morning]]] [153] for Standfast Dick and a drop every minute for Stumblestone Davy]]; scruboak beads for beatified Biddy: two appletweed stools for Eva Mob-

TEXT E

bely: for [[Saara]] Philpot a jordan vale [[[tearorne]]]: a pretty box of pettyfib's powder for Eileen [[[Aruna]]]¹⁵⁴ to whiten her teeth and outflash Helen Arhone: a whippingtop for Eddy Lawless: for Kitty Coleraine of [Butterman's] Lane a penny wise for her foolish pitcher: a putty shovel for [Terry]¹⁵⁵ the Puckaun: a potamus mask for Promoter Dunne: a [[neister]]¹⁵⁶ egg [[with a twicedated shell and a dynamight right]] for [[Pavl]] the Curate; [[a collera morbous for Mann in the Cloack; a starr and girton for Draper and Deane; for Will-of-the Wisp and Barny the Bark two mangolds noble to sweeden their bitters; for Oliver Bound a way in the frey; for Seumas, thought little, a crown he feels big]]; a tibertine's pile with a Congoswood cross on the back for Sunny [[Twimjim]]:¹⁵⁷ [a [[praises]]¹⁵⁸ be and spare me days for Brian the Bravo]; [[[penteplenty]]]¹⁵⁹ [[of pity with [[[lubilashings]]]¹⁶⁰ of lust for [[[Olona]]]¹⁶¹ Lena Magdalena]]; for Camilla, Dromilla, Ludmilla, Mamilla, a bucket, a packet, a book and a pillow: for Nancy Shannon a [[Tuami]] brooch: for Dora [[Riparia]] Hopeandwater a cooling douche and a warmingpan: a pair of Blarney [[braggs]]¹⁶² for Wally Meagher: a hairpin slatepencil for Elsie Oram to scratch her toby, doing her best with her volgar fractions: an old age pension for Betty [[Bellezza]]:¹⁶³ a bag of the blues for Funny Fitz: [[a *Missa pro Messa* for Taff de Taff]]; Jill, the spoon of a girl, for Jack, the broth of a boy: a Rogerson Crusoe Friday fast for Caducus Angelus Rubiconstein: three hundred and sixtysix poplin tyne for revery warp in the weaver's woof for Victor Hugonot: a [stiff¹⁶⁴ steaded] rake and good [varians] muck for Kate the Cleaner: a hole in the ballad for Hosty: two dozen of cradles for J.F.X.P. Coppinger: [[tenpomten on the pop for the daulphins born with five spoiled squibs for Infanta]]: a letter to last a lifetime for Maggy¹⁶⁵ beyond by the ashpit: the heftiest frozenmeat woman from Lusk to Livienbad for Felim the Ferry: spas and speranza [[and symposium's syrup]] for [[decayed and blind and]] gouty Gough: a change of naves and joys of ills for Armoricus Tristram Amoor Saint Lawrence [a guillotine shirt for Reuben Redbreast and hempen suspendeats for Brennan on the Moor]; [[an oakanknee for Conditor Sawyer and musquodoboits for Tropical Scott]]; a C_3 peduncle for Karmalite Kane: a sunless

ANNA LIVIA PLURABELLE

map of the month, including the sword and stamps for Shemus O'Shaun the Post: a jackal with hide for Browne but Nolan: a stonecold shoulder for Donn Joe Vance: all lock and no stable for Honorbright Meretrix: a big drum for Billy Dunboyne: [a guilty goldeny bellows, below me blow me for Ida Ida and a hushaby rocker Elletrouvetout for Who is silvier — Where is he?]:[166] whatever you like to swilly to drink, Yuinness or Yennessy, [[[Laagen]]] or Niger, for Festus King and Roaring Peter and Frisky Shorty and Treacle Tom and O. B. Behan and Sully the Thug and Master Magrath and Peter Cloran [[and O'Delawarr Rossa and Nerone]] [[[MacPacem]]][167] and whoever you chance to meet knocking around: and a bladder balloon for Selina [[Susquehanna]] Stakelum. But what did she give to Pruda Ward [and Katty Kanel] and Peggy Quilty and [Briery] Brosna and Teasy Kieran and Ena Lappin [and Muriel Mosel] [[and [[[Zusan]]][168] Camac and Melissa Bradogue]] and Flora Ferns and Fauna Fox-Goodman [[[and Lezba Licking and Leytha Liane]]] and [[[Una Bina Laterza]]] and Trina La Mesme and Philomena O'Farrell and Irmak Elly and Josephine Foyle and Snakeshead Lily and Fountainoy Laura and Mary Xavier Agnes Daisy Francis de Sales [[[Macleay]]]?[169] She gave them [[[ilcka madre's]]] daughter a moonflower and a [[[bloodvein: but the grapes that ripe before reason to them that divide the vinedress]]]. So on Izzy, her shamemaid, love shone befond her tears as from Shem, her penmight, life past befoul his prime.

My colonial, [[wardha]] bagful! That's what you may call a tale of a tub. All that and more under one crinoline envelope if you dare to break the porkbarrel seal. No wonder they'd run from her [pison] plague. Throw us your hudson soap for the honour of Clane. The wee taste the water left. [[I'll raft it back, first thing in the marne.]] [[[Merced mulde!]]] [[Ay, and don't forget the reckitts I [[[lohaned]]][170] you.]] You've all the swirls your side of the current. Well, am I to blame for that if I have? Who said you're to blame for that if you have? [Only [[snuffers']]][171] cornets drifts my way that the [[crackad dvine]][172] chucks out of his cassock, [[with her[173] estheryear's marsh narcissus to make him recant his vanitty fair.]] Foul strips of his chinook's bible I do be reading, [[dodwell disgustered

TEXT E

but]], chickled with chuckles. *Senior ga dito Faciasi Omo. Omo fu fo.* Ho! Ho! *Senior ga dito: Faciasi Hidamo! Hidamo se ga facessà!* Ha! Ha! And *Die Windermere Dichter* and Lefanu (Sheridens) Old House by the [[Coachyard]] [174] and Mill (J) On Woman with Ditto on the Floss. [[[Ja]]],[175] a swamp for [[[Altmuehler]]] [176] and a stone for his flossies.] [177] [[I know [178] how racy they move his wheel.]] My hands are [[blawcauld]] between [[isker]] and [[[suda]]] [[like]] that piece of pattern chayney there, lying below. Or where is it? Lying beside the [sedge] [179] I saw it. Hoangho, my sorrow, I've lost it! [[[Aimihi!]]] With that [turbary] [180] water who could see? But O, [gihon]! I [[[lovat]]] a gabber. I could listen to maure and [[[moravar]]] again. [[[Regn]]] [181] onder river. Flies do your float. Thick is the life for mere.

Well, you know or don't you [[kennet]] or haven't I told you every [[[telling]]] has [[[a taling]]] and that's the he and the she of it. Look, look, the dusk is growing [[[My branches lofty are taking root. And my cold cher's gone ashley.]]] [182] [[Fieluhr? Filou!]] What [[age]] is [[at]]? It [[saon is]] late. [['Tis endless]] now since I or anyone last saw Waterhouse's [[[clogh]]].[183] They took it asunder, I heard them say. When will they reassemble it? O, my back, my back, my back! I'd want to go to Aches-les-Pains. Wring out the clothes! Wring in the dew! [[Godavari vert the showers! And grant [[[Thaya]]] [184] grace. Aman.]] Will we spread them here now? Ay, we will. Spread on your bank and I'll spread mine on mine. It's what I'm doing. Spread! It's churning chill. Der went is rising. I'll lay a few stones on the [[hostel]] sheets. A man and his bride embraced between them. Else I'd have sprinkled and folded them only. And I'll tie my butcher's apron here. It's suety yet. The strollers [185] will pass it by. Six shifts, ten kerchiefs, [[nine to hold to the fire and this for the code]],[186] the convent [187] napkins twelve, one baby's shawl. [[[Wharnow]]] are [[[alle]]] her childer, [[[say]]]? [[In kingdome gone or power to come or gloria be to them farther? Allalivial, allalluvial!]] Some here, more no more, more again lost [[[alla]]] stranger I've heard tell that same brooch of the Shannons was married into a family in Spain. And all the [Dunders de] Dunnes [in Markland's Vineland] beyond Brendan's [herring pool] takes num-

ANNA LIVIA PLURABELLE

ber nine in [yangsee's] hats. And one of Biddy's beads went bobbing till she rounded up [[[lost]]] histereve with a marigold and a cobbler's candle in a [[side strain of a]] main drain [[of a manzinahurries]] off Bachelor's Walk. But all that's left to the last of the Meaghers [188] [in the [[[loup]]]] [189] of the years prefixed and between] is one kneebuckle and two hooks in the front. Do you tell me that now? I do in troth. [[[Orara por Orbe and poor Las Animas! [190] Ussa, Ulla, we're umbas all! Mezha]]],[191] [didn't you hear it a deluge of times? You deed, you deed! I [[need]],[192] I] [[need]]! [193] [[It's that irrawaddyng I've [[[stoke]]] [194] in my aars. It all but husheth the lethest sound.]] Oronoko! What's [your] [195] trouble? Is that the great Finnleader himself in his joakimono on his statue riding the high horse there forehengist? [Father of Otters, it is himself!] [[Yonne]] there! [[[Isset]]] that? On Fallareen Common? [[You're thinking of Astley's Amphitheayter where the bobby restrained you making sugarstuck pouts [196] to the ghostwhite horse of the Peppers.]] Throw the cobwebs from your eyes, woman, and spread your washing proper. It's well I know your sort of slop. [Ireland sober is Ireland stiff. Your prayers.] Were you lifting your elbow, tell us, glazy cheeks, in [[Conway's]] Carrigacurra canteen? Was I what, hobbledyhips? Amn't I up since the damp dawn with [[Corrigan's pulse and]] varicose veins, soaking and bleaching boiler rags, and sweating cold, a widow like me, [[for]] to deck my tennis champion son, the laundryman with the lavender flannels? [You won your [[limpopo]] limp from the [[husky]] [197] hussars when Collars and Cuffs was heir to the town and your slur gave the stink to Carlow.] Holy Scamander, I [[[sar]]] [198] it again! Near the golden falls. Icis on us! [[Seints of light!]] [[[Zezere!]]] Subdue your noise, you poor creature! What is it but a [[blackburry]] growth or the dwyergray ass them four old codgers owns. Are you [[meanam]] Tarpey and Lyons and Gregory? I mean now, thank all, the four of them, and the roar of them, that [[draves]] that stray in the mist and old Johnny Mac Dougal along with them. Is that the Poolbeg flasher beyant or [[a fireboat coasting]] [[[nyar]]] the [[Kishtna]] or a glow I behold within a hedge [[or my Garry come back from the Indes]]? Wait till the [[honeying]] of the [[lune, love! Die eve, little eve, die! We see

TEXT E

that wonder in your eye.]] [199] [We'll meet again, we'll part once more. The spot I'll seek if the hour you'll find. [[My chart shines]] [200] high where the blue milk's upset.] [[Forgivemequick, I'm going!]] [[[Bubye!]]] [And [[you, pluck]] [201] your watch, forgetmenot.] [[[Your evenlode. So save [202] to jurna's end!]]] My sights are swimming thicker on me by the shadows to this place. [[[I]]] sow home slowly now by own way, moyvalley way. [[[Towy]]] [203] I too, rathmine.

Ah, but she was the queer old skeowsha anyhow, Anna Livia, [[trinkettoes]]! [204] And sure he was the [[quare]] old buntz too, Dear Dirty Dumpling, foostherfather of fingalls [205] and dotthergills. Gammer and gaffer we're all their gangsters. Hadn't he seven dams to wive him? And every dam had her seven crutches. And every crutch had its seven hues. And each hue had a differing cry. [Sudds], for me and supper for you and the doctor's bill for Joe John.[206] Before! Before! He married his markets, cheap by foul, I know, [like any Etrurian Catholic Heathen, in their pinky limony creamy [[birnies]] and their turkiss indienne mauves]. But at milkidmass who was the spouse? Then all that was was fair. [[[Tys]]] Elvenland? Teems of times and happy returns. The [[[seim]]] anew. Ordovico or viricordo. Anna was, Livia is, Plurabelle's to be. Northmen's thing made southfolk's place but howmulty plurators made eachone in person? Latin me that, my trinity scholard, [out of [[[eure]]] [207] sanscreed into [[[oure]]] [208] eryan]. *Hircus Civis Eblanensis!* He had buckgoat paps on him, soft ones for orphans. Ho, Lord! Twins of his bosom. Lord save us! And ho! Hey? What all men. Hot? His tittering daughters of. Whawk?

Can't hear with the waters of. The chittering waters of. Flittering bats, fieldmice bawk talk. Ho! Are you not gone ahome? What Tom Malone? Can't hear with bawk of bats, all the liffeying waters of. Ho, talk save us! My foos won't moos. I feel as old as yonder elm. A tale told of Shaun or Shem? All Livia's daughtersons. Dark hawks hear us. Night! Night! My ho head halls. I feel as heavy as yonder stone. Tell me of John or Shaun? Who were Shem and Shaun the living sons or daughters of? Night now! Tell me, tell me, tell me, elm! Night night! Tell me tale of stem or stone. Beside the rivering waters of, hitherandthithering waters of. Night! [209]

↑ ↑ ↑ ↑ ↑ ↑ TEXT F

O T E L L me all about Anna Livia! I want to hear all about Anna Livia. Well, you know Anna Livia? Yes, of course, we all know Anna Livia. Tell me all. Tell me now. You'll die when you hear. Well, you know, when the old cheb went futt and did what you know. Yes, I know, go on. Wash [quit] and don't be dabbling.[1] Tuck up your sleeves and loosen your talktapes. [And don't butt me—hike!—when you bend.] Or whatever it was they [threed] to make out he [thried] to [two] in the Fiendish park. He's an awful old [reppe]. Look at the shirt of him! Look at the dirt of it! He has all my water black on me. And it steeping and stuping since this time last [[wik]]. How many goes is it I wonder I washed it? I know by heart the places he likes to saale, duddurty devil! Scorching my hand and starving my famine to make his private linen public. Wallop it well with your battle and clean it. My wrists are [rwusty] rubbing the mouldaw stains. And the dneepers of wet and the gangres of sin in it! What was it he did a tail at all on Animal Sendai? And how long was he under [[loch]] and neagh? It was put in the [newses] what he did, nicies and priers, the King fierceas Humphrey, with illysus distilling, exploits and all. But toms will [till]. I know he [well]. Temp untamed will hist for no man. [[As you spring so shall you neap.]] O, the roughty old [rappe! Minxing[2] marrage and making loof. Reeve Gootch was right and Reeve Drughad[3] was] [[[sinistrous]]]![4] And the cut of him! And the strut of him! How he used to hold his head as high as a howeth, the famous eld duke alien, with a hump of grandeur on him

NOTE: This text is a composite of the Gaige galleys, the Gaige ALP, and the Faber ALP; emendations on the Gaige galleys are enclosed in single brackets, those on Joyce's postulated corrections of the later galleys in double brackets, those between the Gaige ALP and the Faber ALP in triple brackets.

TEXT F

like a walking rat. And his derry's own drawl and his corksown blather and his doubling stutter and his gullaway swank. Ask Lictor Hackett or Lector Reade or Garda Growley or the Boy with the Billyclub. How elster is he a called at all. Qu'appelle? Huges Caput Earlyfouler? Or where was he born or how was he found? Urgothland, Tvistown on the Kattekat? New Hunshire, Concord on the Merrimake? Was her banns never loosened in Adam and Eve's [[or]] were him and her [[but captain]] spliced? [[For mine ether duck I thee drake. And by my wildgaze I thee gander.]] Flowey and Mount on the brink of time makes wishes and fears for a happy isthmass. O, passmore that and oxus another! Don Dom Dombdomb and his wee follyo! [[Was his help inshored in the Stork and Pelican against bungelars, flu and third risk parties?]] I heard he dug good tin with his doll when he raped her home, Sabrine asthore, in a parakeet's cage, by dredgerous lands and devious delts, playing catched and mythed with the gleam of her shadda, past auld min's manse and Maisons Allfou and the rest of incurables and the last of immurables, the quaggy waag for stumbling. Who sold you that jackalantern's tale? [[Pemmican's pasty pie!]] In a gabbard he barqued it, the boat of life, from the harbourless Ivernikan Okean, till he spied the loom of his landfall and he loosed two croakers from under his tilt, the gran Phenician rover. By the smell of her kelp they made the pigeonhouse. Like fun they did! But where was Himself, the timoneer? That marchantman he [[suivied]] their scutties right over the wash, his cameleer's burnous breezing up on him, till with his runagate bowmpriss he roade and borst her bar. Pilcomayo! Suchcaughtawan! And the whale's away with the grayling! Tune your pipes and fall ahumming, you born ijypt, and you're nothing short of one! Well, ptellomey soon and curb your [[escumo]]. When they saw him shoot swift up her sheba sheath, like any gay lord salomon, her bulls they were ruhring, surfed with spree. Boyarka buah! Boyana bueh! He erned his lille Bunbath hard, our staly bred, the trader. He did. Look at here. In this wet of his prow. Don't you know he was kalled a bairn of the brine, Wasserbourne the waterbaby? Havemmarea, so he was. H.C.E. has a [codfiscck][5] ee. Shyr she's [[near]] as badher as him herself. Who? Anna Livia? Ay, Anna

ANNA LIVIA PLURABELLE

Livia. Do you know she was calling backwater sals from all around to go in till him, her erring [[cheef]], and tickle the pontiff aisy-oisy? She was? Gota pot! Well, that's the limmat! As El Negro [winced] when he [wonced] in La Plate. O, tell me all I want to hear, [[how loft she was lift a laddery dextro! A coneywink after the bunting fell.]] Letting on she didn't care, the proxenete! Proxenete and phwhat[6] is phthat? Tell us in franca langua. [[And call a spate a spate.]] Did they never sharee you ebro at skol, you antiabecedarian? It's just the same as if I was to go for examplum now out of telekinesis and proxenete you. For coxyt[7] sake and is that what she is? Botlettle I thought she'd act that loa. Didn't you spot her in her windaug, wubbling up on an osiery chair, with a meusic before her all cunniform letters, pretending to ribble a reedy derg on a fiddle she bogans without a band on? Sure she can't fiddan a dee, with bow or abandon! [[[Sure]]],[8] she can't! Tista suck. Well, I never heard the[9] like of that! Tell me [[moher]]. Tell me [moatst]. Well, old Humber was as glommen as grampus, with the tares at his thor and the buboes for ages and neither bowman nor shot abroad and bales [[allbrant]] on the crests of rockies and nera lamp in kitchen or church and giant's holes in Grafton's causeway, [[[sittang]]] sambre on his benk, drammen and [[[drommen]]], his childlinen scarf to encourage his obsequies, where he'd check their debths in that mormon's thames, [[be questing and handset, hop, step and a deepend, with his berths in their toiling moil, his swallower open from swolf to fore and the snipes of the gutter pecking his crocs]], hungerstriking all alone and holding doomsdag over [[hunselv]], dreeing his weird, with his dander up, and his fringe combed over his eygs and droming on loft till the sight of the sternes, after zwarthy kowse and weedy broeks and the tits of buddy and the loits of pest and to peer was Parish worth thette mess. You'd think all was dodo belonging to him how he durmed adranse in durance vaal. He had been belching for severn years. And there she was, Anna Livia, she darent catch a winkle of sleep, purling around like a chit of a child, in a Lapsummer skirt and damazon cheeks, for to ishim bonzour to her dear dubber Dan. With neuphraties and sault from his maggias. And an odd time she'd cook him up blooms of fisk and lay to his

TEXT F

heartsfoot her meddery eygs and staynish beacons on toasc and a cupenhave so weeshywashy of Greenland's tay or a dzoupgan of Kaffue mokau [[an sable]] or Si-kiang sukry or his ale of ferns in trueart pewter and a shinkobread for to plaise that man hog stay his stomicker till her pyrraknees shrunk to nutmeg graters and as rash as she'd russ with her peakload of vivers up on her sieve (his towering rage it swales and [rieses]!)[10] my hardey Hek he'd kast them frome him, with a stour of scorn, as much as to say you sow and [11] you sozh, and if he didn't peg the platteau on her tawe, believe you me, she was safe enough. And then she'd esk to vistule a hymn, *The Heart Bowed Down* or *The Rakes of Mallow* or Chelli Michele's *La Calumnia è un Vermicelli* or a balfy bit [[[ov]]] *old Jo Robidson*. Sucho fuffing a fifeing 'twould cut you in two! She'd bate the hen that crowed on the turrace of Babbel. What harm if she knew how to cockle her mouth. And not a mag out of Hum no more than out of the mangle weight. Is that a faith? That's [[the]] fact. Then [riding] the ricka and roya romanche, Annona, gebroren aroostokrat Nivia, [dochter [12] of Sense and Art], with Sparks' pirryphlickathims funkling her fan, [anner] [[frostivying]] tresses dasht with virevlies, — while the prom beauties sreeked [[nith]] their bearers' skins! — in a period gown of changeable jade that would robe the wood of two cardinals' chairs and crush poor Cullen and smother MacCabe. [[O blazerskate! Theirs porpor patches!]] And brahming to him down the feedchute, with all kinds of fondling endings, the poother rambling off her nose: *Vuggybarney, Wickerymandy! Hello, ducky, please don't die!* Do you know what she started cheeping then, [with a [[choicey]] voicey] like [[waterglucks]]? You'll never guess. Tell me. Tell me. *Phoebe, dearest, tell, O tell me* and *I loved you better nor you knew*. And letting on [hoon var] daft about the warbly sangs from over holmen: *High hellskirt saw ladies hensmoker lilyhung pigger*: and soay and [soan and so firth and so forth] in a tone sonora and Oom Bothar below in his sandy cloak, so umvolosy, as deaf as a yawn, [[the stult]]! Go away! Poor deef old deary! Yare only [[teasing]]! [13] Anna Liv? As chalk is my judge! And didn't she up [in] [[sorgues]] [14] and go and trot doon and stand in her douro, puffing her old dudheen, and every shirvant siligirl or wensum farm-

ANNA LIVIA PLURABELLE

erette walking the pilend roads Sawy, Fundally, Daery or Maery, Milucre, Awny or Graw, usedn't she make her a simp or sign to slip inside by the sullyport? You don't say the sillypost? I did. And do. Calling them in one by one (To Blockbeddum here! Here the Shoebenacaddie!) and legging a jig or so on the sihl to show them how to shake their benders and the dainty how to bring to mind the gladdest garments out of sight and all the way of a maid with a man and making a sort of a [15] cackling noise like two and a penny or half a crown and holding up a silliver shiner. Lordy, lordy, did she so? Well, of all the ones ever I heard! Throwing all the neiss little whores in the world at him! To inny captured wench you wish of no matter what sex of pleissful ways two adda tammar a lizzy a lossie to hug and hab haven in Humpy's apron!

And what was the wyerye rima she made! [Odet! Odet!] Tell me the trent of it while I'm lathering hail out of Denis Florence MacCarthy's combies. [Rise it, flut ye, pian piena!] I'm dying down off my iodine feet until I [lerryn] Anna Livia's cushingloo! I can see that, I see you are. How does it tummel? Listen now. Are you listening? Yes, yes! Idneed I am! Tarn your ore ouse. Essonne inne.

By earth and the cloudy but I badly want a brandnew bankside, bedamp and I do, and a plumper at that!

For the putty affair I have is wore out, so it is, sitting, yaping and waiting for my old Dane [[hodder]] *dodderer, my life in death companion, my frugal key of our larder, my much-altered camel's hump, my jointspoiler, my maymoon's honey, my fool to the last Decemberer, to wake himself out of his winter's doze and bore me down like he used to.*

Is there irwell a lord of the manor or a knight of the shire at [strike], *I wonder, that'd dip me a pound or two in cash for washing and darning his worshipful socks for him now we're run out of horsemeat and milk?*

Only for my short Brittas bed [[[made's]]] *as snug as it smells it's out I'd lep and offwith me to the slobs* [[della]] *Tolka or the* [[plage au]] *Clontarf to feale the gay aire of my salt troublin bay and the race of the saywint up me ambushure.*

Onon! Onon! tell [16] me more. Tell me every tiny teign. I want to

TEXT F

know every single ingul. Down to what made the potters fly into jagsthole. And why were the vesles vet. Well, now comes the hazelhatchery part. After Clondalkin the Kings's Inns. We'll soon be there with the freshet. How many aleveens had she in tool? I can't rightly [rede] you that. Close only knows. Some say she had three figures to fill and confined herself to a hundred eleven, [wan] [[bywan bywan]].[17] [Olaph lamm et, all that pack? We won't have room in the kirkeyaard.] She can't remember half of the cradlenames she smacked on them by the grace of her boxing bishop's infallible slipper, [the cane for Kund and abbles for Eyolf and ayther nayther for Yakov Yea]. A hundred and how? They did well to rechristien her [[Pluhurabelle]]. O loreley! What a loddon [[lodes! Heigh ho! But it's quite on the the cards she'll shed more and merrier, twills and trills, sparefours and spoilfives, nordsihkes and sudsevers and ayes and neins to a litter. Grandfarthring nap and Messamisery and the knave of all knaves and the joker. Heehaw!]] [18] She must have been a gadabount in her day, so she must, more than most. Shoal she was, gidgad. She had a flewmen of her owen. [Then a toss nare scared that lass, so [19] aimai moe, that's agapo!] Tell me, tell me, how cam she camlin through all her fellows, the neckar she was, the diveline? Linking one and knocking the next, tapting a flank and tipting a jutty and palling in and pietaring out and clyding by on her eastway. Waiwhou was the first thurever burst? Someone he was, whuebra they were, in a tactic attack or in single combat. Tinker, tilar, souldrer, salor, Pieman Peace or Polistaman. That's the thing I always want to know. Push up and push upper and come to headquarters! Was it waterlows year, after Grattan or Flood, or when maids were in Arc or when three stood hosting? Fidaris will find where the Doubt arises like Nieman [20] from Nirgends found the Nihil. Worry you sighin foh, Albern, O Anser? Untie the gemman's fistiknots, [Qvic] and Nuancee? She can't put her hand on him for the moment. Tez thelon langlo, walking weary! Such a loon way backwards to row! She says herself she hardly knows whuon the annals her graveller was, a dynast of Leinster, a wolf of the sea, or what he did or how blyth she played or [[how]], when, [[why]], where and [[who offon]] he [[[jumpnad]]] [21] her. She was just a young thin pale soft shy slim

ANNA LIVIA PLURABELLE

slip of a thing then, sauntering, [by silvamoonlake] [22] and he was a heavy trudging lurching lieabroad of a Curraghman, making his hay for [whose] sun to shine on, as tough as the oaktrees (peats be with them!) used to rustle that time down by the dykes of killing Kildare, [[for]] forstfellfoss with a plash across her. She thought [she's] [23] sankh neathe the ground with nymphant shame when he gave her the tigris eye! O happy fault! Me wish it was he! You're wrong there, corribly wrong! Tisn't only tonight you're anacheronistic! It was ages behind that when nullahs were nowhere, in county Wickenlow, garden of Erin, before she ever dreamt she'd lave Kilbride and go foaming under Horsepass bridge with the great southerwestern windstorming her traces and the midland's grainwaster asarch for her track, to wend her ways byandby, [robecca] or worse, to spin and to grind, to swab and to thrash, [for all her golden lifey] in the barleyfields and pennylotts of Humphrey's fordofhurdlestown and lie with a landleaper, wellingtonorseher. [[Alesse]], the [[lagos]] of girly days! For the dove of the dunas! Wasut? Izod? Are you [[sarthin]] suir? Not where the Finn fits into the Mourne, not where the Nore takes lieve of Blœm, not where the Braye divarts the Farer, not where the Moy changez her minds twixt Cullin and Conn tween Cunn and Collin? Neya, narev, nen and nos! Then whereabouts in Ow and Ovoca? Was it yst with wyst or Lucan Yokan or where the hand of man has never set foot? Dell me where, the [fairy] ferse time! I will if you listen. You know the dinkel dale of Luggelaw? Well, there once dwelt a local heremite, Michael Arklow was his riverend name, (with many a sigh I aspersed his lavabibs!) and one venersderg in junojuly, oso sweet and so cool and so limber she looked, Nance the Nixie, Nanon L'Escaut, in the silence, of the sycomores, all listening, the [[kindling]] curves you simply can't stop feeling, he plunged both of his newly anointed hands to [the core of] his cushlas in her singimari saffron strumans of hair, parting them and soothing her and mingling it, that was deepdark and ample like [this] red bog at sundown. [By that Vale Vowclose's lucydlac, the reignbeau's heavenarches arronged orranged her. Afrothdizzying [24] galbs, her enamelled eyes indergoading him on to the vierge violetian. Wish a wish! Why a why? Mavro! Letty Lerck's

TEXT F

lafing light throw those laurals now on her daphdaph teasesong petrock.] Maass! He cuddle not help himself, thurso that hot on him, he had to forget the monk in the man so, rubbing her up and smoothing her down, he baised his lippes in smiling mood, kiss akiss after kisokushk (as he warned her never to, never to, never) on Anna-na-Poghue's of the freckled forehead. While you'd parse secheressa she hielt her [souff'. But she ruz two feet hire [25] in her aisne aestumation. And steppes on stilts ever since.] O, wasn't he the bold priest? And wasn't she the naughty Livvy? Nautic Naama's now her navn. Two lads in [[[scoutsch]]] breeches went through her before that, Barefoot Burn and [[Wallowme]] Wade, Lugnaquillia's [[noblesse]] [[[pickts]]],[26] before she had a hint of a hair at her fanny to hide or a bossom to tempt a birch canoedler not to mention a [[bulgic]] porterhouse [27] barge. And ere that again, [[leada, laida]], all [[unraidy]], too faint to buoy the fairiest rider, too frail to flirt with a cygnet's plume, she was licked by a hound, Chirripa-Chirruta, while poing her pee, pure and simple, on the spur of the hill in old Kippure, in birdsong and shearingtime, but first of all, worst of all, the wiggly livvly, she sideslipped out by a gap in the Devil's glen while Sally her nurse was sound asleep in a sloot and, [[feefee fiefie]], fell over a spillway before she found her stride and lay and wriggled in all the stagnant black pools of rainy under a fallow coo and she laughed innocefree with her limbs aloft and a whole drove of maiden hawthorns blushing and looking askance upon her.

Drop me the sound of the findhorn's name. And drip me why in the flenders was she frickled. And trickle me through was she marcellewaved or was it weirdly a wig she wore. And whitside did they droop their glows in their florry, aback to wist or affront to sea? In fear to hear the dear so near or longing loth and loathing longing? Are you in the swim or are you out? O go [in], go on, go [an]! I mean about what you know. I know right well what you mean. [Rother!] You'd like the coifs and guimpes, snouty, and me to do the greasy jub on old Veronica's [wipers]. What am I rancing now and I'll thank you? Is it a pinny or is it a surplice? Arran, where's your nose? And where's the starch? That's not the vesdre benediction smell. I can tell from here by their *eau de Colo* and the scent of

ANNA LIVIA PLURABELLE

her oder they're Mrs Magrath's. And you ought to have aird them. They've moist come off her. Creases in silk they are, not crampton lawn. Baptiste me, father, for she has sinned! Through her catchment ring she freed them easy, with her hips'hurrahs for her knees'-dontelleries. The only [[parr]] with frills in old the plain. So they are, [I declare]! Welland well! [If tomorrow keeps fine who'll come tripping to sightsee? [[How'll? ²⁸ Ask]] ²⁹ me next what I haven't got! The Belvedarean exhibitioners.] [[In their sculling caps and oarsclub colours.]] [What hoo, they band! And what hoa, they buck!] And here is her nubilee letters too. Ellis on quay in scarlet thread. Linked for the world on a flushcoloured field. Annan exe after to show they're not Laura Kehoe's. O, may the diabolo twisk your seifety pin! You child of Mammon, Kinsella's Lilith! Now who has been tearing the leg of her drawers on her? Which leg is it? The one with the bells on it. Rinse them out and aston along with you. Where did I stop? Never stop. Continuarration! You're not there yet. Garonne, garonne!

Well, after it was put in the [[Mericy Cordial Mendicants']] Sitterdag-Zindeh-Munaday Wakeschrift (for once they sullied their white [kidloves], [[chewing cuds after their dinners of cheeckin and beggin]], with their show us it here and their mind out of that and their when you're quite finished with the reading matarial), even the snee that snowdon his hoaring hair had a skunner against him. Thaw, thaw, sava, savuto! [[Score Her Chuff Exsquire!]] Everywhere erriff you went and every bung you arver dropped into, in cit or [[suburb]] or in [addled] areas, the Rose and Bottle or Phoenix Tavern or Power's Inn or Jude's Hotel, or wherever you scoured the countryside from Nannywater to Vartryville or from Porta Lateen to the lootin quarter you found his ikom etched tipside down or the cornerboys burning his guy and Morris the Man, with the role of a royss in his turgos the turrible, (Evropeahahn cheic house, unskimmed sooit and yahoort, [[hamman]] now cheekmee, Ahdahm this way make, Fatima, half turn!) reeling and railing [[[round]]] the local with oddfellow's triple tiara busby rotundarinking round his scalp. Like Pate-by-the-Neva or Pete-over-Meer. This is the Hausman all paven and stoned, that cribbed the Cabin that never

TEXT F

was owned, that cocked his leg and hennad his Egg. And the mauldrin rabble around him in areopage, [[fracassing]] a great [bingkan] [[cagnan]] with their timpan crowders. Mind your Grimmfather! Think of your Ma! [Hing the Hong is his jove's hangnomen! Lilt a bolero, bulling a law!] She swore on croststyx [[nyne wyndabouts]] she'd be level with all the snags of them yet. Par the Vulnerable Virgin's Mary del [Dame]! So she said to herself she'd frame a plan to fake a shine, the mischiefmaker, the like of it you niever heard. What plan? Tell me quick and dongu so crould! What the meurther did she mague? Well, she bergened a bag, a shammy mailbag, off one of her swapsons, Shaun the Post, and then she went and consulted her chapboucqs, old Mot Moore, Casey's Euclid and the Fashion Display and made herself tidal to join in the mascarete. O [[gig]] goggle of gigguels. I can't tell you how! It's too screaming [to rizo], rabbit it all! [[Minneha, minnehi minaaehe, minneho!]] O but you must, you must really! [[Make my hear it gurgle gurgle, like the farest gargle gargle in the dusky dirgle dargle!]] By the holy well of Mulhuddart I swear I'd pledge my chanza getting to heaven [[through Terry and Killy's mount of impiety]] to hear it all, [[aviary]] word. O, leave me my faculties, woman, a while. If you don't like my story, get out of the punt. Well, have it your own way, so. Here, sit down and do as you're bid. [[Take my stroke and bend to your bow. Forward in and pull your overthepoise!]] Lisp it slaney and crisp it quiet. Deel me longsome. Tongue your time now. Breathe thet deep. Thouat's the fairway. Hurry slow and scheldt you go. Lynd us your blessed ashes here till I scrub the canon's underpants. Flow now. Ower more.

First she let her hair fall and down it flussed to her feet its teviots winding coils. Then, mothernaked, she sampood herself with galawater and fraguant [pistania] mud, wupper and lauar, from crown to sole. Next she greased the groove of her keel, warthes and wears and mole and itcher, with antifouling [butterscatch] and [[turfentide]] [30] and serpenthyme and with leafmould she ushered round prunella isles and islets dun, [[quincecunct, allover]] her little mary. [[Peeld gold of waxwork her jellybelly and her grains of incense anguille bronze.]] And after that she wove a garland for her

ANNA LIVIA PLURABELLE

hair. She pleated it. She plaited it. Of meadowgrass and riverflags, the bulrush and waterweed, and of fallen griefs of weeping willow. Then she made her bracelets and her anklets and her armlets and a jetty amulet for necklace of clicking cobbles and pattering pebbles and rumbledown rubble, richmond and rehr, of Irish [[rhunerhinerstones]] [31] and shellmarble bangles. That done, a dawk of smut to her airy ey, [[Annushka Lutetiavitch Pufflovah]], and the lellipos cream to her lippeleens and the pick of the paintbox for her pommettes, from strawbirry reds to extra [32] violates, and she sent her boudeloire maids to His Affluence, Ciliegia Grande and Kirschie Real, the two chirsines, with respecks from his missus, seepy and sewery, and a request she might [[passe of]] him for a minnikin. A call to pay and light a taper, in Brie-on-Arrosa, back in a sprizzling. The cock striking mine, the stalls bridely sign, there's Zambosy waiting for me. She said she wouldn't be half her length away. Then, then, as soon as the lump his back was turned, with her mealiebag slang over her [shulder], Anna Livia, oysterface, forth of her bassein came.

Describe her! Hustle along, why can't you? Spitz on the iern while it's hot. I wouldn't miss her for irthing [on nerthe]. Oceans of [Gaud], I mussel hear that! [[Ogowe presta!]] [Leste, before Julia sees her!] Ishekarry and washemeskad, the carishy caritimaney? [[Whole lady fair? [33] Duodecimoroon? Bon a ventura? Malagassy?]] What had she on, the liddel [oud] oddity? How much did she scallop, harness and weights? Here she is. Amnisty Ann. Call her calamity electrifies man.

No electress at all, but old Moppa Necessity, [[angin]] mother of [[injons]]. I'll tell you [[a test]]. But you must sit still. Will you hold your peace and listen well to what I am going to say now? It might have been ten or twenty to one of the night of Allclose or the nexth of April when the flip of her hoogly igloo flappered and out [[toetippit]] a [[bushman]] woman, the dearest little moma ever you saw, nodding around her, all smiles, with ems of embarras and aues to awe, between two ages, a judyqueen, not up to your elb. [[Quick]], look at her [cute] and [saise] her quirk for the bicker she lives the slicker she grows. Save us and tagus! No more? Werra where in ourthe did you ever pick a Lambay chop as big as a battering ram?

TEXT F

Ay, you're right. I'm epte to forgetting, Like Liviam Liddle did Loveme Long. The linth of my hough, I say! She wore a ploughboy's nailstudded clogs, a pair of ploughfields in themselves: a sugarloaf hat with a gaudyquiviry peak and a band of gorse for an arnoment and a hundred streamers dancing off it [34] and a [[guildered]] pin to pierce it: owlglassy bicycles boggled her eyes: and a fishnetzeveil she had to keep the sun from spoiling her wrinkles: potatorings boucled the loose laubes of her [laudsnarers]: her nude cuba stockings were salmospotspeckled: she sported a galligo shimmy of hazevaipar tinto that never was fast till it ran in the washing: stout stays, the rivals, lined her length: her bloodorange bockknickers, a two in one garment, showed natural nigger boggers, fancyfastened, free to undo: her blackstripe tan joseph was sequansewn and teddybearlined, with wavy rushgreen epaulettes and a leadown here and there of royal swansruff: a brace of gaspers stuck in her hayrope garters: her civvy codroy coat with alpheubett buttons was boundaried round with a twobar tunnel belt: a fourpenny bit in each pocketside weighed her safe from the blowaway windrush; she had a clothespeg tight astride [[on]] her joki's nose and she kep on grinding a sommething quaint in her fiumy mouth and the rrreke of the fluve of the tail of the gawan of her snuffdrab siouler's skirt trailed ffiffty Irish miles behind her lungarhodes.

Hellsbells, I'm sorry I missed her! Sweet gumptyum and nobody fainted. But in whelk of her mouths? Was her naze alight? Everyone that saw her said the dowce little delia looked a bit queer. Lotsy trotsy, mind the poddle! Missus, be good and don't fol in the say! Fenny poor hex she must have charred. Kickhams a frumpier ever you saw. Making saft mullet's eyes at her boys dobelong. And they crowned her [their] chariton queen, [all the maids]. Of the may? You don't say! Well for her she couldn't see herself. I recknitz [wharfore] the darling murrayed her mirror. She did? Mersey me! There was a koros of drouthdropping surfacemen, boomslanging and plugchewing, fruiteyeing and flowerfeeding, in contemplation of the fluctuation and the undification of her filimentation, lolling and leasing on [North Lazers'] Waal [all eelfare week] by the Jukar Yoick's and as soon as they saw her meander by [that marritime way] in her

ANNA LIVIA PLURABELLE

grasswinter's weeds and twigged who was under her deaconess bonnet, Avondale's fish and Clarence's poison, sedges an to [aneber],[35] Wit-upon-Crutches to Master Bates: *Between [our two southsates]* [36] *and the granite [they're] warming, [[or her face has been lifted or]] Alp has doped.*

But what was the game in her mixed baggyrhatty? And where in thunder did she plunder? Fore the battle or efter the ball? I want to get it frisk from the soorce. I aubette my [[bearb]] it's worth while poaching on. Shake it up, do, do! That's a good old son of a ditch! I promise. I'll make it worth your while. And I don't mean maybe. [[Nor yet with a goodfor.]] Spey me pruth and I'll tale you true.

Well, [arundgirond] in a waveney lyne aringarouma she pattered and swung and sidled, dribbling her boulder through narrowa mosses, the diliskydrear on our drier side and the vilde vetchvine agin us, curara here careero there, not knowing which [37] medway or [[weser]] to strike it, edereider, making chattahoochee all to her ain chichiu, like Santa Claus at the cree of the pale and puny, nistling to hear for their tiny hearties, her arms encircling Isolabella, then running with reconciled [Romas] and [Reims], then bathing Dirty Hans' spatters with spittle, with a Christmas box apiece for aisch and iveryone of her childer, the birthday gifts they dreamt they gabe her, [the spoiled she fleetly laid at our door.[38] On the matt,[39] by the pourch and inunder the cellar.] [40] The rivulets ran [aflod] [41] to see, the glashaboys, the pollynooties. Out of the [paunschaup] on to the pyre. And they all about her, youths and maidens, rickets and riots, like the Smyly boys at their vicereine's levee. Vivi vienne, little [Annchen, vielo] Anna,[42] high life! Sing us a sula, O, susuria! [[Ausone sidulcis!]] Hasn't she tambre! Chipping her and raising a bit of a chir or a jary every [[dive]] she'd neb in her culdee sacco of wabbash she raabed and reach out her maundy [meerschaundize, poor souvenir as per [[ricorder]] [43] and all for sore aringarung], stinkers and heelers, laggards and primelads, her furzeborn sons and dribblederry daughters, a thousand and one of them, and wickerpotluck for each of them. For evil and ever. And kiks the buch. A tinker's bann and a barrow to boil his billy for Gipsy Lee; a cartridge of cockaleekie soup for Chummy the Guardsman; for sulky Pender's

TEXT F

acid nephew deltoïd drops, curiously strong; a cough and a rattle and wildrose cheeks for poor [Piccolina] Petite MacFarlane; a jigsaw puzzle of needles and pins and blankets and shins between them for Isabel, Jezebel and Llewelyn [Mmarriage]; a brazen nose and pigiron mittens for Johnny Walker Beg; a [papar] flag of the saints and stripes for Kevineen O'Dea; a puffpuff for Pudge Craig and a nightmarching hare for Techer Tombigby; waterleg and gumboots each for Bully Hayes and Hurricane Hartigan; a prodigal heart and fatted calves for Buck Jones, the pride of Clonliffe; a loaf of bread and a father's early aim for Tim from Skibereen; a jauntingcar for Larry Doolin, the Ballyclee jackeen; a seasick trip on a government ship for Teague O'Flanagan; a louse and trap for Jerry Coyle; slushmincepies for Andy Mackenzie; a hairclip and clackdish for Penceless Peter; that twelve sounds look for G. V. Brooke; a drowned doll, [[to face downwards]] for [[modest]] Sister Anne Mortimer; altar falls for Blanchisse's bed; Wildairs' [[breechettes]] for Magpeg [[Woppington]]; to Sue Dot a big eye, to Sam Dash a false step; [[snakes]] in clover, [picked and scotched], and a vaticanned vipercatcher's visa for Patsy Presbys; a [reiz] every morning for Standfast Dick and a drop every minute for Stumblestone Davy; scruboak beads for beatified Biddy; two appletweed stools for Eva Mobbely; for Saara Philpot a jordan vale tearorne; a pretty box of Pettyfib's Powder for Eileen Aruna to whiten her teeth and outflash Helen Arhone; a whippingtop for Eddy Lawless; for Kitty Coleraine of Butterman's Lane a penny wise for her foolish pitcher; a putty shovel for Terry the Puckaun; a [[[apotamus]]] mask for Promoter Dunne; a niester egg with a twicedated shell and a dynamight right for Pavl the Curate; a collera morbous for Mann in the Cloack; a starr and girton for Draper and Deane; for Will-of-the-Wisp and Barny the Bark two mangolds noble to sweeden their bitters; for Oliver Bound a way in [his] frey; for Seumas, thought little, a crown he feels big; a tibertine's pile with a Congoswood cross on the back for Sunny Twimjim; a praises be and spare me days for Brian the Bravo; penteplenty of pity with lubilashings of lust for Olona Lena Magdalena; for Camilla, Dromilla, Ludmilla, Mamilla, a bucket, a packet, a book and a pillow; for Nancy Shannon a Tuami brooch; for Dora

ANNA LIVIA PLURABELLE

Riparia Hopeandwater a cooling douche and a warmingpan; a pair of Blarney braggs for Wally Meagher; a hairpin slatepencil for Elsie Oram to scratch her toby, doing her best with her volgar fractions; an old age pension for Betty Bellezza; a bag of the blues for Funny Fitz; a *Missa pro Messa* for Taff de Taff; Jill, the spoon of a girl, for Jack, the broth of a boy; a Rogerson [Crusoe's] Friday fast for Caducus Angelus Rubiconstein; three hundred and sixtysix poplin tyne for revery warp in the weaver's woof for Victor Hugonot; a stiff steaded rake and good varians muck for Kate the Cleaner; a hole in the ballad for Hosty; two dozen of cradles for J.F.X.P. Coppinger; [tenpounten] on the pop for the daulphins born with five spoiled squibs for Infanta; a letter to last [44] a lifetime for Maggi beyond by the ashpit; the heftiest frozenmeat woman from Lusk to Livienbad for Felim the Ferry; spas and speranza and symposium's syrup for decayed and blind and gouty Gough; a change of naves and joys of ills for Armoricus Tristram Amoor Saint Lawrence; a guillotine shirt for Reuben Redbreast und hempen suspendeats for Brennan on the Moor; an oakanknee for Conditor Sawyer and musquodoboits for [[Great]] Tropical Scott; a C_3 [45] peduncle for Karmalite Kane; a sunless map of the month, including the sword and stamps for Shemus O'Shaun the Post; a jackal with hide for Browne but Nolan; a stonecold shoulder for Donn Joe Vance; all lock and no stable for Honorbright Meretrix; a big drum for Billy Dunboyne; a guilty goldeny bellows, below me blow me for Ida Ida and a hushaby rocker Elletrouvetout for Who-is-silvier — Where-is-he?; whatever you like to swilly to [swash],[46] Yuinness or Yennessy, Laagen or Niger, for Festus King and Roaring Peter and Frisky Shorty and Treacle Tom and O. B. Behan and Sully the Thug and Master Magrath and Peter Cloran and O'Delawarr Rossa and Nerone MacPacem and [47] whoever you chance to meet knocking around; and a [[pig's]] bladder balloon for Selina Susquehanna Stakelum. But what did she give to Pruda Ward and Katty Kanel and Peggy Quilty and Briery Brosna and Teasy Kieran and Ena Lappin and Muriel Mosel and Zusan Camac and Melissa Bradogue and Flora Ferns and Fauna Fox-Goodman [and Grettna Greaney and Penelope Inglesante] and Lezba Licking [like][48] Leytha Liane

TEXT F

[and Roxana Rohan with Simpatica Sohan] and Una Bina Laterza and Trina La Mesme and Philomena O'Farrell and Irmak Elly and Josephine Foyle and Snakeshead Lily and Fountainoy Laura and [[Marie]] Xavier Agnes Daisy [[Frances]] de Sales Macleay? She gave them ilcka madre's daughter a moonflower and a bloodvein: but the grapes that ripe before reason to them that devide [49] the vinedress. So on Izzy, her shamemaid, love shone befond her tears as from Shem, her penmight, life past befoul his prime.

My colonial, wardha bagful! [[A bakereen's dusind with tithe tillies to boot.]] That's what you may call a tale of a tub. All that and more under one crinoline envelope if you dare to break the porkbarrel seal. No wonder they'd run from her pison plague. Throw us your hudson soap for the honour of Clane. The wee taste the water left. I'll raft it back, first thing in the marne. Merced mulde! Ay, and don't forget the reckitts I lohaned you. You've all the swirls your side of the current. Well, am I to blame for that if I have? Who said you're to blame for that if you have? [You're a bit on the sharp side. I'm on the wide.] Only snuffers' cornets drifts my way that the cracka [50] dvine chucks out of his cassock, with her estheryear's marsh narcissus to make him recant his vanitty fair. Foul strips of his chinook's bible I do be reading, dodwell disgustered but chickled with chuckles [[at the tittles is drawn on the tattlepage]]. *Senior ga dito: Faciasi Omo!* [[[*E*]]] *omo fu fò.* Ho! Ho! *Senior ga dito: Faciasi Hidamo! Hidamo se ga facessà.* Ha! Ha! And *Die Windermere Dichter* and Lefanu [[[(Sheridan's)]]] [51] Old House by the Coachyard and Mill (J.) On Woman with Ditto on the Floss. Ja, a swamp for Altmuehler and a stone for his flossies. I know how racy they move his wheel. My hands are blawcauld between isker and suda like that piece of pattern chayney there, lying below. Or where is it? Lying beside the sedge I saw it. Hoangho, my sorrow, I've lost it! Aimihi! With that turbary water who could see? [So near and yet so far!] But O, gihon! I lovat a gabber. I could listen to maure and moravar again. Regn onder river. Flies do your float. Thick is the life for mere.

Well, you know or don't you kennet or haven't I told you every telling has a taling and that's the he and the she of it. Look, look,

ANNA LIVIA PLURABELLE

the dusk is growing. My branches lofty are taking root. And my cold cher's gone ashley. Fieluhr? Filou! What age is at? It saon is late. 'Tis endless now since [eye] or [[erewone]] [52] last saw Waterhouse's clogh. They took it asunder, I [[hurd]] [thum sigh]. When will they reassemble it? O, my back, my back, my [bach]! I'd want to go to Aches-les-Pains. [Pingpong! There's the Belle for [[Sexaloitez]]! [53] And Concepta de Send-us-pray! Pang!] Wring out the clothes! Wring in the dew! Godavari, vert the showers! And grant thaya grace! Aman. Will we spread them here now? Ay, we will. [Flip!] Spread on your bank and I'll spread mine on mine. [Flep!] It's what I'm doing. Spread! It's churning chill. Der went is rising. I'll lay a few stones on the hostel sheets. A man and his bride embraced between them. Else I'd have sprinkled and folded them only. And I'll tie my butcher's apron here. It's suety yet. The strollers will pass it by. Six shifts, ten kerchiefs, nine to hold to the fire and this for the code, the convent napkins twelve, one baby's shawl. [[Good mother Jossiph knows, she said. Whose head? Mutter snores? Deataceas!]] Wharnow are alle her childer, say? In kingdome gone or power to come or gloria be to them farther? Allalivial, allalluvial! Some here, more no more, more again lost alla stranger. I've heard tell that same brooch of the Shannons was married into a family in Spain. And all the Dunders de Dunnes in Markland's Vineland beyond Brendan's herring pool takes number nine in yangsee's hats. And one of Biddy's beads went bobbing till she rounded up lost histereve with a marigold and a cobbler's candle in a side strain of a main drain of a manzinahurries off Bachelor's Walk. But all that's left to the last of the Meaghers in the loup of the years prefixed and between is one kneebuckle and two hooks in the front. Do you tell me that now? I do in troth. Orara por Orbe and poor Las Animas! Ussa, Ulla, we're umbas all! Mezha, didn't you hear it a deluge of times, [[ufer and ufer, respund to spond]]? You deed, you deed! I need, I need! It's that irrawaddyng I've stoke in my aars. It all but husheth the lethest sound. Oronoko! What's your trouble? Is that the great Finnleader himself in his joakimono on his statue riding the high horse there forehengist? Father of Otters, it is himself! Yonne there! Isset that? On Fallareen Com-

TEXT F

mon? You're thinking of Astley's Amphitheayter where the bobby restrained you making sugarstuck pouts to the ghostwhite horse of the Peppers. Throw the cobwebs from your eyes, woman, and spread your washing proper. It's well I know your sort of slop. [Flap!] Ireland sober is Ireland stiff. [Lord help you, Maria, full of grease, the load is with me!] Your prayers. [[I sonht zo! Madammangut!]] Were you lifting your elbow, tell us, glazy cheeks, in Conway's Carrigacurra canteen? Was I what, hobbledyhips? [Flop! Your rere gait's [[creakorheuman]] [54] [[bitts]] [55] your] [[butts [56] disagrees]].[57] Amn't I up since the damp dawn, [marthared mary allacook] with Corrigan's pulse and [[varicoarse]] [58] veins, [my pramaxle smashed, Alice Jane in decline and [[my oneeyed]] [59] mongrel twice run over], soaking and bleaching boiler rags, and sweating cold, a widow like me, for to deck my tennis champion son, the laundryman with the lavender flannels? You won your limpopo limp from the husky hussars when Collars and Cuffs was heir to the town and your slur gave the stink to Carlow. Holy Scamander, I sar it again! Near the golden falls. Icis on us! Seints of light! Zezere! Subdue your noise, you [hamble] creature! What is it but a blackburry growth or the dwyergray ass them four old codgers owns. Are you meanam Tarpey and Lyons and Gregory? I [meyne] now, thank all, the four of them, and the roar of them, that draves that stray in the mist and old Johnny MacDougal along with them. Is that the Poolbeg flasher beyant, [pharphar], or a fireboat coasting nyar the Kishtna or a glow I behold within a hedge or my Garry come back from the Indes? Wait till the honeying of the lune, love! Die eve, little eve, die! We see that wonder in your eye. We'll meet again, we'll part once more. The spot I'll seek if the hour you'll find. My chart shines high where the blue milk's upset. Forgivemequick, I'm going! Bubye! And you, pluck your watch, forgetmenot. Your evenlode. So save to jurna's end! My sights are swimming thicker on me by the shadows to this place. I sow home slowly now by own way, moyvalley way. Towy I too, rathmine.

Ah, but she was the queer old skeowsha anyhow, Anna Livia, trinkettoes. And sure he was the quare old buntz too, Dear Dirty Dumpling, foostherfather of fingalls and dotthergills. Gammer and

ANNA LIVIA PLURABELLE

gaffer we're all their gangsters. Hadn't he seven dams to wive him? And every dam had her seven crutches. And every crutch had its seven hues. And each hue had a differing cry. Sudds for me and supper for you and the doctor's bill for Joe John. [[Befor! Bifur!]] He married his markets, cheap by foul, I know, like any Etrurian Catholic Heathen, in their pinky limony creamy birnies and their turkiss indienne mauves. But at milkidmass who was the spouse? Then all that was was fair. Tys Elvenland? Teems of times and happy returns. The seim anew. Ordovico or viricordo. Anna was, Livia is, Plurabelle's to be. Northmen's thing made southfolk's place but howmulty plurators made eachone in person? Latin me that, my trinity scholard, out of eure sanscreed into oure eryan. *Hircus Civis Eblanensis!* He had buckgoat paps on him, soft ones for orphans. Ho, Lord! Twins of his bosom. Lord save us! And ho! Hey? What all men. Hot? His tittering daughters of. Whawk?

Can't hear with the waters of. The chittering waters of. Flittering bats, fieldmice bawk talk. Ho! Are you not gone ahome? What Tom Malone? Can't hear with bawk of bats, all the liffeying waters of. Ho, talk save us! My foos won't moos. I feel as old as yonder elm. A tale told of Shaun or Shem? All Livia's daughtersons. Dark hawks hear us. Night! Night! My ho head halls. I feel as heavy as yonder stone. Tell me of John or Shaun? Who were Shem and Shaun the living sons or daughters of? Night now! Tell me, tell me, tell me, elm! Night night! [[[Telmetale]]] of stem or stone. Beside the rivering waters of, hitherandthithering waters of. Night! [60]

*TEXTUAL APPENDIX, NOTES, AND
BIBLIOGRAPHICAL NOTE*

TEXTUAL APPENDIX

THE following list includes all changes made in the text between the Faber ALP and FW. Usually, first appearance only is cited. The numbers at the left refer to page and line number of FW. Four dots mean more than one sentence.

196.17 *wrusty*: without apparent authority; thus FW only.
197.04 *wiesel*: 47475.77b.
197.07 *of*: without apparent authority; set 47476A.119 and succeeding texts.
197.11 *Who . . . pail?*: 47475.77b.
197.15 *She . . . may!*: 47475.77b; 166b has *eje* for eye.
197.20 *delvan . . . after*: 47475.77b.
197.23 *(if . . . him!)*: 47475.77b.
197.27 *Not . . . ore.*: 47475.78a; *antsgrain* orig. *antsweight*.
198.07 *kaldt*: without apparent authority; thus FW only.
198.11 *bakvandets*: 47475.78a.
198.11 *nyumba . . . choo*: 47476A.262.
198.13 *Yssel that*: 47475.78a.
198.16 *sina . . . passession*: 47476A.263.
198.18 *Emme . . . jarkon*: 47475.78b; here *reussischer's*, copied (47475.-167b) by amanuensis as *reussischer*; 78b: *jarkon* orig. foll. by comma and *mam*.
198.21 *par*: 47475.78b.
198.21 *in . . . cause*: 47475.78b.
198.27 *now*: 47476A.120.
198.32 *and . . . occumule*: 47475.78b, which has *ocummule*; 167b: *occumule*.
198.34 *sett*: 47475.78b
198.35 *usking . . . continence*: 47475.78b.
199.01 *handsetl*: without apparent authority; thus FW only.
199.12 *Wendawanda, a fingerthick*: 47476A.263.
199.16 *yayis*: 47476A.263.
199.20 *(hamjambo, bana?)*: 47476A.263.
199.21 *while . . . goyt*: 47475.79a.
199.23 *metauwero*: 47475.79a.
200.05 *her femtyfyx*: 47475.79b.
200.08 *after*: 47475.79b.
200.09 *or . . . Romeoreszk*: 47475.79b.
200.14 *like Bheri-Bheri*: 47475.79b.
200.22 *Bedouix but*: 47475.79b.
201.01 *that . . . parco*: 47475.80a.
201.14 *dace*: 47475.80a.

ANNA LIVIA PLURABELLE

201.16 *horsebrose*: 47475.80b.
201.23 *That* . . . . *askarigal*: 47476A.265.
201.30 *making meanacuminamoyas*: 47476A.265.
202.08 *Casting* . . . *tilhavet*: 47475.81a (with *From*); 170a: *from*.
202.15 *I'm* . . . *esk*: 47475.81a; *on* foll. by strikeout, poss. *Ach*.
202.16 *vardar*: 47475.81a.
202.16 *uphill*: 47475.81a.
202.22 *waybashwards*: 47475.81a; 170a: *werrabackwoods* (amanuensis).
202.23 *sid*: 47475.81a.
202.26 *and* . . . *away*: 47475.81a.
203.12 *Or* . . . *two?*: 47476A.123.
203.14 *nonni*: 47475.81b.
203.23 *to* of Text F: omitted between galleys and Gaige ALP.
203.31 *But* . . . . *slewd*: 47476A.266.
203.36 *niver, nevar*: 47475.82a.
204.03 *That* . . . *balm*: 47476A.267.
204.21 *Mtu* . . . *wisness*: 47476A.267.
205.06 *cruisery*: without apparent authority; thus FW only.
205.08 *flush-caloured*: without apparent authority; thus FW only.
205.09 *Keown's*: without apparent authority; thus FW only.
205.12 *drawars*: 47475.83a.
205.14 *I* . . . *waiting*: 47475.83a.
205.28 *cammocking*: 47475.83a.
205.32 *as* . . . *twanged*: 47475.83a.
206.05 *she's*: without apparent authority; set 47476A.125 and succeeding texts.
206.09 *zakbag*: 47475.83b; here simply *zak*; amanuensis copies (47475.172b) as *zakbag*.
206.10 *mailsack*: 47475.83b.
206.10 *with* . . . *lampion*: 47476A.125.
206.19 *Tirry*: without apparent authority; thus FW only.
206.28 *And pooleypooley*: 47476A.268.
206.29 *fal*: 47475.84a.
206.35 *eslats*: 47475.84a.
207.11 *sendred*: 47475.84b.
207.22 *Not* . . . *strait*: 47475.84b.
207.23 *mosel*: 47475.84b.
208.10 *for* . . . *hydeaspects*: 47475.85a.
208.26 *odd*: 47475.85b.
208.32 *mush*: 47475.85b.
208.33 *dobelon*: 47475.85b.
209.06 *archdeaconess*: 47476A.127.
209.07 *sedges*: 47475.85b; 174b: *wheezes* (amanuensis); 85b: orig. *sid*.
209.10 *Just* . . . . *bizaas*: 47476A.270.
209.25 *on* . . . *dart*: 47475.86a.
209.32 *juvenile* . . . *wellings*: 47475.86a; here *artesans dwelling*; changed (47475.175a) to *artesaned wellings*.
210.15 *Techertim*: without apparent authority; thus FW only.
210.18 *Val*: without apparent authority; thus FW only.
210.25 *breechettes*: without apparent authority; thus FW only.
210.35 *an*: without apparent authority; thus FW only.
211.11 *braggs*: 47475.87a: altered to *tweedbags* and marked stet.

TEXTUAL APPENDIX

211.33 *Merreytrickx*: 47475.87b.
212.08 *Maassy*: without apparent authority; thus FW only.
212.21 *And . . . market*: 47475.88a; here *Hibernian* and with the addition of *too* at the end; corrected (47475.177a) to *Hibernonian*; *too* omitted when set at 47476A.130.
213.15 *senne*: 47475.88b.
214.10 *zswound*: 47475.89b.
214.28 *lavandier*: 47475.89b.
215.33 *thim*: without apparent authority; thus FW only.

NOTES

Notes to Text A*

[1] 74a: orig. *did* for bracketed passage. [2] 74a: struck out, but recurs in succeeding text. [3] 73b: orig. *he*; foll. by strikeout *was born at.* [4] 74a: orig. *the window*, foll. by strikeout *playing.* [5] 74a: orig. *the grand piano* for bracketed passage. [6] 74a: orig. *piano.* [7] 74a: [sic]; possibly a false start. [8] 74a: orig. *anything* for bracketed passage. [9] 73b: *staring* is crossed out; *his hair . . . eyes* may be intended to follow *sternes*; here in order of Text B.
[10] 74a: foll. by strikeout *and a powdery nose.* [11] 73b: *–ng* crossed out; orig. *cooking.* [12] 73b: orig. *all sorts.* [13] 73b: orig. *bring* for *run with.* [14] 73b: orig. *the.* [15] 74a: orig. *budge.* [16] 74a: orig. probably *Singing.* [17] 73b: foll. by strikeout *of his long ago. High Yay.* [18] 73b: foll. by strikeout *do.* [19] 73b: orig. *go* for bracketed passage.
[20] 73b: orig. *passed* for bracketed passage. [21] 75a: orig. *do.* [22] 75a: foll. by strikeout *and holding up a half a crown and showing them how to bill and coo.* [23] 74b: orig. *dancing.* [24] 74b: foll. by strikeout *in silver.* [25] 74b: orig. *coin* for *silver shiner.* [26] 75a: foll. by strikeout *to any girl.* [27] 75a: orig. *make.* [28] 74b: orig. *plump one.* [29] 74b: orig. *one* for *putty affair.*
[30] 74b: foll. by strikeout *doing nothing.* [31] 74b: orig. *the.* [32] 74b: orig. *Dansker* for *Dane the dodderer.* [33] 74b: orig. *pantry.* [34] 74b: foll. by strikeout *hump of her.* [35] 74b: orig. *faithful*; then *true to the last*; then *fool to the last* for preceding four words. [36] 74b: orig. *dumps.* [37] 74b: foll. by strikeout *at me.* [38] 74b: foll. by strikeout *old chap.* [39] 74b: preceding three words are written over what is probably either *of the land* or *of the head.*
[40] 74b: orig. *soft job*; then *few pounds*; then *pound or two.* [41] 74b: orig. *shirts.* [42] 74b: orig. *everything* for *meat and milk.* [43] 74b: written over an illegible word, possibly *so.* [44] 74b: orig. *be.* [45] 74b: orig. *the.* [46] 75a: orig. *single thing.* [47] 75a: orig. *call.* [48] 75a: orig. *never.* [49] 75a: possibly *when.*
[50] 75a: foll. by addition *and miles*; but see succeeding texts. [51] 75a: orig. *thought.* [52] 76a: two preceding words may be *his pennyland.* [53] 76a: orig. poss. *She.* [54] 76a: possibly *are.* [55] 76a: *You . . . glen* written over *There was a holy hermit.* [56] 76a: orig. *July.* [57] 76a: orig. *put his two* for preceding six words. [58] 76a: orig. *time after time again* for bracketed passage. [59] 75b: orig. *Jack.*
[60] 75b: orig. *the summertime.* [61] 75b: orig. *wall.* [62] 75b: foll. by strikeout *down.* [63] 75b: orig. *bungh.* [64] 77a: orig. *loose.* [65] 76b: orig. *painted beautyspots* for *multiplied moles.* [66] 76b: written over *on*; foll. by another *all* and strikeout *her skin.* [67] 77a: foll. by strikeout *of.* [68] 77a: *–tones* crossed out. [69] 77a: orig. *gems.*
[70] 77a: orig. *bag.* [71] 77a: orig. *is.* [72] 77a: orig. *know.* [73] 77a: orig. *came.* [74] 77a:

* All page numbers refer to B. M. Add. MS 47471B.

NOTES

preceding three words crossed out; but see succeeding texts. [75] 77a: orig. *broadbottomed*. [76] 76b: foll. by strikeout *of*. [77] 77a: orig. *screening*. [78] 78a: orig. *in* for bracketed passage. [79] 78a: foll. by strikeout *add her* or *and her*.
 [80] 78a: orig. *with* for bracketed passage. [81] 78a: orig. *belted with* for bracketed passage. [82] 78a: foll. by strikeout, probably *so as she*. [83] 78a: orig. *old brown*. [84] 76b: poss. *McCormick*. [85] 77b: *Brown B* only struck out. [86] 77b: the parenthesis also contains *An D* struck out; the parenthesis is written in Irish script. [87] 77b: first word possibly *Laog*.

Notes to Text B *

[1] 78b: The *it* is probably a reconstructed *h*. [2] 78b: *And was he ever spliced*; then *And were he and she ever spliced*; then *And were him and her ever spliced*. [3] 79a: orig. *he is*. [4] 79a: orig. *to go into* for bracketed passage. [5] 80a: foll. by strikeout *up*. [6] 79b: foll. by strikeout *Wickerwacky!*. [7] 80a: orig. *lily*. [8] 82a: [sic]. [9] 83a: foll. by strikeout *once*.
 [10] 82b: orig. *Ireland*; then *Newireland*; then *Ereleinster*; then *Orkney*. [11] 84a: struck out. [12] 84a: orig. *name*. [13] 84a: orig. *cow* for *shorthorn's name*. [14] 83b: orig. *the old chap's*. [15] 83b: orig. *rolling*. [16] 83b: orig. *head*. [17] 84b: foll. by strikeout *go*. [18] 84b: orig. *combinations*. [19] 85a: *washed herself* omitted in copying.
 [20] 86a: written over *to*. [21] 86a: orig. *owlglasses*, before addition of *bicycles*. [22] 86a: addition foll. also by comma. [23] 87a: orig. *or other* for bracketed passage. [24] 87a: orig. *snuffbrown*; then *snuffcoloured*; then *snuffdrab*. [25] First draft ends here; brackets in remainder of Text B mark "original" emendations. [26] 87a: struck out. [27] 87a: foll. by strikeout *what*. [28] 87a: foll. by strikeout *She must have looked a funny poor dear*. [29] 86b: orig. *dear*.
 [30] 86b: poss. *surfaceman*. [31] 86b: strikeout for preceding five words is either *seen them* or *seen these*. [32] 86b: orig. *we're on* for *beneath us*. [33] 87a: order of preceding four sentences as indicated in MS. [34] 87a: orig. *children*. [35] 87a: orig. *bag*. [36] 87a: orig. *brass badge* for bracketed passage. [37] 87a: orig. *Babbs*; then *Baby*; then *Bubsy*. [38] 87a: orig. probably *Beggar*. [39] 87a: orig. *a waterleg*. [40] 88a: orig. *Big Bully*. [41] 88a: orig. *a*. [42] 88a: orig. *child's bladder*. [43] 87b: orig. *Hope*. [44] 87b: orig. *in*. [45] 87b: orig. *the Clonliffe boy* for preceding four words. [46] 87b: punctuation is poss. a comma. [47] 87b: foll. by another *for* in MS. [48] 88a: foll. by strikeout *and Nancy Shann*. [49] 88a: orig. *moonflowers* for preceding two words.
 [50] 88a: foll. by strikeout *O'Gorman*. [51] 88a: orig. *life*. [52] 88a: orig. *son*. [53] 88a: orig. *Give me*. [54] 88a: foll. by strikeout *it's growing*. [55] 89a: struck out. [56] 88a: orig. *gone* for bracketed passage. [57] 89a: foll. by strikeout *at all*. [58] 88b: orig. *a*. [59] 88b: orig. *fellows*.
 [60] 88b: struck out; no verb supplied. [61] 89a: orig. *one*. [62] 89a: orig. *hunks*. [63] 88b: foll. by strikeout *Furry Humphrey*. [64] 88b: written over another *us*. [65] 89a: orig. *big*. [66] 89a: struck out. [67] 89a: foll. by strikeout *The Lord save us and bless us!* and; there is a phrase in the margin of the MS, *twins of his chest*, but the entire passage is so heavily corrected that it is impossible to tell where the phrase was to be inserted. [68] 89a: orig. *The*; then *O*; then *Ho*. [69] 89a: orig. *The*.
 [70] 89a: foll. by strikeout, probably *have*. [71] 89a: foll. by strikeout *him. Amen*; *Bawk* is written in the margin of the MS at this point. The next paragraph appears to have orig. begun with *I*, which is struck out. [72] 89a: struck out and

---

* All page numbers refer to B. M. Add. MS 47471B.

ANNA LIVIA PLURABELLE

reinserted. [73] 89a: orig. *Is that Mrs Malone* for bracketed passage. [74] 89a: orig. *and*. [75] 90a: orig. *or*. [76] 90a: orig. *and*. [77] When a word or phrase which appears in Text B is omitted from Text C, it may be assumed that Joyce did not insert it on the fair copy.

Notes to Text C *

[1] Bracketed passage added on last page of first typescript of preceding chapter, 47474.36b; *he likes to soil* orig. *he soils*; *sewers* orig. *tons*. [2] 125: *what*. [3] 125: orig. *why* for *how long*. [4] 125: *It*. [5] 107: foll. by strikeout *awful*. [6] 125: orig. *carted*. [7] 125: foll. by strikeout *Devil a*. [8] 125: orig. *told*. [9] 125: *his*. [10] 125: typed, without apparent authority. [11] 125: *a*. [12] 126: typed, without apparent authority. [13] 127: first marked to read *fisk to lay at his feet and meddery*; then as here. [14] 108: orig. *the*. [15] 108: there is a mark in the text at this point as if *Phoebe* to *me* (v. below) was orig. to have been added here; the phrase is preceded by strikeout *and*. [16] 108: in fair copy only. [17] 108: orig. *falling from* for *rambling off*. [18] 127: foll. by mark indicating addition. [19] 108: *camel* (struck out) *old warbly*; *old* not copied on typescript.

[20] 109: the word may be *sallyport*; but Joyce does not correct the typescript, which reads as here. [21] 109: orig. *all*. [22] 128: typed *ir* and altered as here. [23] 128: typed *Purabelle* and altered as here. [24] 119: foll. by *Well*. [25] 119: orig. *backwards*. [26] 119: *O so* for *Such a*. [27] 129: *saunfering*. [28] 119: orig. *stout*. [29] 129: *Killing*; 111 as here.

[30] 111: foll. by strikeout *Tell*. [31] 119: foll. by *they say*; 111 as here. [32] 119: *bright and*; 111 as here. [33] 119: foll. by strikeout *rubbing* to *down* (v. below). [34] 129: *couln't*. [35] 130: *Naughtnaughty*. [36] 130: typed, without apparent authority. [37] 130: *side-slipped*. [38] 130: *spillwas*. [39] 120: orig. *in all the [rain] stagnant black rainpools [of]* for bracketed passage; brackets in note indicate strikeouts.

[40] 130: *I am* for *am I*. [41] orig. *sacristy*. [42] 129b: this addition and the following one in double brackets appear here in Joyce's hand, but they also appear typed on 130. [43] 129b: *there's* in Joyce's hand; 130: *there is*; and cf. succeeding texts. [44] 129: orig. *her*. [45] 112: foll. by comma; 130: comma omitted on typescripts; and cf. succeeding texts. [46] 120: *it*; 112 as here. [47] 112: *everywhere*, with no pn. preceding. [48] 131: *fropped*. [49] 131: *cronerboys*.

[50] 132: *Pet*. [51] 132: foll. by period. [52] 113: foll. by comma; 132: foll. by period; cf. succeeding texts. [53] 132: orig. *tell*. [54] 132: end pn. *?*. [55] 113: *from her crown to her sole*; both *hers* struck out on 132. [56] 113: foll. by strikeout *the*. [57] 113: *an*. [58] 132: *pebble*. [59] 113: foll. by strikeout *rumblin*.

[60] 132: typed *rummledown* and altered. [61] 132: *of*. [62] 133: bracketed passage orig. as Text B. [63] 114: end pn. written over *!*. [64] 133: *salmonspotspeekled*. [65] 133: orig. *wash*. [66] 115: foll. by strikeout *she held*. [67] 133: orig. *well*, preceded by strikeout *It was*. [68] 115: foll. by strikeout *And*. [69] 115: probably *every one*.

[70] 115: orig. *children*. [71] 115: orig. *out with* for brackets, as Text B. [72] 134: *cockaleekine*. [73] 115: orig. *for Pender's sulky nephew acid drops* from preceding colon. [74] 116: orig. *petite*. [75] 121: orig. *mitts*. [76] 134: typed *Waterleg* and altered; cf. the "Boy McCormick" phrase of Text B. [77] 121: *waterleg* to *Harti-*

* All page numbers refer to B. M. Add. MS 47474. Sheets of revised fair copy are 119–123; the complete fair copy is 107–118; the typescript is 125–138.

NOTES

gan marked to follow *Beg*, above; here and for certain other phrases (v. 78, 80, 82, 89), the order followed is that of the typescript and 116. [78] 121: *a jauntingcar* to *jackeen* marked to follow *O'Flanagan*, below. [79] 121: *trial*; 116: orig. *trial*.

[80] 121: *mudmincepies* to *Mackenzie* marked to follow *Brook*, below. [81] 121: *haircut*; 116: *hairclip*. [82] 121: *Brook*; *a hairclip* to *Brook* marked to follow *Lucky Joe*, below. [83] 121: *Holy*; 116: *holy*. [84] 135: *Alamah*. [85] 135: bracketed passage added in typing, without apparent authority. [86] 116: orig. *coolish douche*. [87] 134b: misread by typist as *Gill*; 135: *Gill*. [88] 134b: preceded by strikeout, probably *Se*. [89] 135: *a stonecold* to *Vance* orig. marked to go here.

[90] 134b: *plenty of*. [91] 134b: foll. by strikeout *Archdea*. [92] 134b: *from here to Howth* for preceding four words. [93] 135: orig. *spawater*, foll. by *and* and strikeout *spes*. [94] 134b: *stars*. [95] 135: orig. *Carmen*; then *Honourbright*; then *Honorbright*. [96] 134b: foll. by strikeout *like*. [97] 135: foll. by strikeouts *Mary* and *Sara*. [98] 135: *Brosua*. [99] 135: typed foll. by *and Lappin*.

[100] 135: bracketed passage added in typing. [101] 116: end pn. period. [102] 136: lacks period; 116 as here. [103] 122: orig. *for*. [104] 122: orig. *for the fish* for *to your float*. [105] 122: foll. by strikeout *I*. [106] 122: foll. by strikeout *it is now. The*. [107] 122: orig. *put*. [108] 122: orig. *slept*. [109] 136: bracketed passage added in typing.

[110] 136: bracketed passage added in typing. [111] 136: *covent*. [112] 117: foll. by comma; 136: lacks comma. [113] 136 lacks period; 117 probably intends a period, which is covered by the loop of a *d* in the following line. [114] 136: *falimy*. [115] 117: *Dunne's*, corr. on 136. [116] 122: orig. *was*. [117] 122: preceded by strikeout *rolling*; foll. by *lonesome*, which 117 omits. [118] 122: *stuck* for *rounded up*. [119] 136: *Meachere*.

[120] 137: *Fallarees*. [121] 137: bracketed passage added in typing. [122] 137: bracketed passage added in typing. [123] 137: *blackburry*; persistent (cf. FW, 214.32); but 117 is plainly *blackberry*. [124] 137: *gorwth*. [125] 137: omits: v. Text D. [126] 123: *night*; 118: orig. *dark*, then *mist*. [127] 137: *Poolbey*. [128] 123: *light*; 118 as here. [129] 137: *mear*.

[130] 137: *Skeowsha*. [131] 123: the *h* of *anyhow* is written over a *w*, as if the orig. intention was *anyway*; 137 omits comma; on 118 it is conflated with the B of *Buntz*. [132] 118: orig. *Buntz*. [133] 123: *dear dirty*; 118 as here. [134] 137: *gangters*. [135] 137: *dan*. [136] 137: *and*. [137] 123: *every*. [138] 123: *Joe John*; 118 as here. [139] 138: orig. *near and far*.

[140] 138: orig. *milkingtime*. [141] 123: *billygoat*; 118 as here. [142] 123: foll. by strikeout *large*. [143] 123: *Yes?*; 118 as here. [144] 123: *What?*; 118 as here. [145] Cf. Text D and note. [146] 138: *ols*. [147] 138: foll. by comma; 118 has no comma, but the stroke of the exclamation point of *Night!*, below, was probably so interpreted by the typist. [148] Change without apparent authority; 118 and 123: *Nighty*; but succeeding texts as here. [149] See Text B, n. 77.

Notes to Text D *

[1] 186: *dug good* and *his doll* appear here only; *tin* appears also on 142.
[2] all typescripts *perokeet's*; galleys and succeeding texts as here, without apparent authority. [3] 143a: orig. *himself*. [4] 143a: *The*; altered 144. [5] 143a:

*All page numbers refer to B. M. Add. MS 47474. Sheets of the second typescript are 160–166; the three copies of the third typescript are 142–159, 168–184, and 186–202; the galleys are 204–206. For the editorial policy in this and following texts, see the Editorial Note.

ANNA LIVIA PLURABELLE

merchantman. [6] 143a: *broke*; altered 144, where *borst* is written over (poss.) *broke*. [7] 143a: *Paleiliou!*; altered on 169 to *Pwllhjllyou!*, then as here. [8] 143a: *idiot*; altered 169 to *ijjit*, then as here. [9] 143a: orig. *it*. [10] 143a: *by*; altered 144. [11] 143b: foll. by strikeout *they the*. [12] 143b: foll. by strikeout *her*. [13] 143b: orig. *Bunbad*. [14] 143b: orig. *well*. [15] 142: *Didn't* and *was*, both crossed out, appear at the bottom of this page, which is cut away; the sentence is retyped as given here on 144; succeeding texts *Don't*. [16] 204: *phwat*, as also *Navire*. [17] 170: typed *to*, without apparent authority. [18] 145: *Cox'*, but succeeding texts as here. [19] 145: altered to *a reedy* for bracketed passage.

[20] 160: orig. *tune*, then *rime*, then *wave*; 145: *wave or two* for bracketed passage. [21] 160: *debts*. [22] 145, 188: *himself*. [23] 160: orig. *at*, then *till*, then *to*. [24] 160: *knees were worn* for bracketed passage. [25] Omitted on all typescripts and galleys; succeeding texts as here. [26] 171: *I did and I do* for preceding two sentences; 204 as here; both emendations in Joyce's hand; 189: *I and do*. [27] 172: *rywye*; but 190 and succeeding texts as here. [28] All typescripts and galleys *I am*; succeeding texts as here. [29] Thus 190 only; but thus also succeeding texts.

[30] 147: *Bull* altered to *strand*; 172 as here. [31] 147: *hole* altered to *ambushore*. [32] 161: *falling*. [33] 161: *falling*. [34] 161: orig. *aven dale*. [35] 161: *rotten*; 173: *corriby*. [36] 161: foll. word *well* altered to *byandby*. [37] 173: *Suir*; but succeeding texts as here. [38] 161: written over illegible word. [39] 173: *venusderg*; but 191 and succeeding texts as here.

[40] From here to *shearingtime* omitted on galleys, which have instructions to supply from third copy. [41] This and following two bracketed words on 192 in Joyce's hand. [42] 149: *on* altered to *down*. [43] 149: orig. *tell*, then *riddle*, then *trickle*. [44] 149: *only* altered to *mostly*. [45] 175: *Ormond* for *O, may*. [46] 205: set *Monthly* and corr. [47] 175, 193: *pixture*; but not in galleys or succeeding texts. [48] 206: *cronerboys*; v. Text C and note. [49] 150: *make*, altered to *fray*; 175: *make*, altered as here; 193: *make*, altered to *fray*, altered to *frame*.

[50] 205: foll. by strikeout *and surfentine*. [51] 173: foll. by strikeout *out*. [52] 151: *of* altered to *or*; v. Text C and note; *of* altered to *and* on 176. [53] All typescripts and galleys *salmospotspeekled*; v. Text C and note; succeeding texts as here. [54] 152: *forty* altered to *sixty*. [55] 178: end pn. *!* in Joyce's hand; 206:.. [56] 162: *looked* altered to *turned*. [57] 153: *soft*; 196: *saft*, without apparent authority; but thus succeeding texts. [58] 162: orig. *muddied*. [59] 162: *by the Royal George* for bracketed passage.

[60] 162: foll. by strikeout *mud and*. [61] This spelling of the word never has any justification in Joyce's hand, but he lets it stand here and in succeeding texts; v. also Text C and note. [62] Thus galleys and succeeding texts without apparent authority; all typescripts *the*. [63] 163: *applewood* altered to *appletreed*; 179: *stools*, not copied on 197; corrected on 206. [64] 163: *outsmile*. [65] 163: *Ellen*. [66] 163: altered from *plenty of*; v. also Text C and note. [67] 164: orig. *names*. [68] 164: orig. *choice*. [69] 164: orig. *Grillroom*.

[70] 164: orig. *Larynx*. [71] 164: foll. by strikeout *and*. [72] Galleys end here; remainder supplied from third copy. [73] 164: orig. *Irma Kelly* and for bracketed passage. [74] 164: foll. by strikeout *so*. [75] 200: bracketed passage in Joyce's hand. [76] 182: *wend*; 200: the *d* of *wend* is struck over with a *t*; thus succeeding texts. [77] 200: *covent*; v. Text C and note. [78] 165: *Meachere* altered to *Meaghere*; 200: *Meaghere*. [79] 182: foll. by *or* in Joyce's hand; but v. succeeding texts.

[80] All typescripts *lavendar*. [81] 201: in Joyce's hand. [82] 166: *go* altered to *so*; 183 as here. [83] 166: *my valley*; altered 183. [84] 166: *Too will I too my mine* for

NOTES

sentence; altered 183. [85] 166: *fotthergills*; but all typescripts as here; and v. succeeding texts. [86] All typescripts *gangters*. [87] 166: orig. *elvenband*. [88] 201: preceding sentence in Joyce's hand. [89] 166: *creators*; altered 158.
[90] 202: *want*; 184: corr. to *won't*; v. Text C for a possible lost emendation. [91] 202: *ols*; corr. 184.

Notes to Text E *

[1] The Yale copy is preceded by a note in Joyce's hand: "This is the final corrected version of *A.L.P.*/Given to Mr James Wells with thanks for/his kind suggestion and generous terms of/publication./J.J." [2] Thus 209 and succeeding texts, without apparent authority; *Navire: week*. [3] Thus also *Navire*. [4] 210: *eld*. [5] 210: comma after *Concord* in Joyce's hand; *transition*: set without comma. [6] 210: *with*. [7] 210: *pass me*. [8] 210: foll. by strikeout *sp*. [9] 210: preceded by strikeout *Sutchcau*.
[10] 211: end pn. period in Joyce's hand; but v. succeeding texts. [11] 211: *phwat*; v. Text D and note. [12] 211: orig. *antiabbecedarian*. [13] 211: *Little*. [14] 211: *low*. [15] 211: *music*. [16] 211: orig. *pest*. [17] 211: foll. by strikeout *a*. [18] 211: foll. by strikeout *score*. [19] 211: orig. *hills*.
[20] 211: *devil a*. [21] 211: poss. intended as *drummen*; cf. Text F. [22] 211: set *kecking*, as also *Navire*; the error persists throughout the typescripts for Text D; but *transition*: *keeking*. [23] 211: set *warthy* and altered. [24] 211: set *brocks*. [25] 211: *the*. [26] 211: orig. *How*. [27] 211: *satt* for bracketed passage. [28] 211: orig. *wish*, then *wiss a*. [29] 211: bracketed passage set between *like* and *a chit*.
[30] 211: orig. *salt*. [31] Yale copy: marked to read *mokau kaffue*. [32] 230: foll. by *and to ile the gules of her old villaine* in Joyce's hand; but v. succeeding texts. [33] 212: *taw*. [34] 212: *Such*. [35] 212: *and*. [36] 212: *queen of queens* for bracketed passage. [37] 212: set *frostifred* and altered as here. [38] 212: *lit*. [39] 212: *fireflies*; 250: *vireflies*; Yale copy as here; 212: foll. phrase has opening dash (not set in *transition*) in Joyce's hand.
[40] 212: orig. *shrieked*, then *shreeked*, then as here. [41] 212: *clothe*. [42] 212: *deery*. [43] 213: orig. *Blackbottom*. [44] 213: *nice*. [45] 213: *and a* altered to *add a*. [46] 213: *alass* for preceding two words. [47] 213: *I am*; v. Text D and note. [48] Thus also *Navire*. [49] 213: *ear*.
[50] 213: orig. *here*. [51] Thus also *Navire*. [52] 213: altered to *Audelle* in Joyce's hand; but v. succeeding texts. [53] *Navire: toll*. [54] *Navire: a hundred and eleven* for preceding three words. [55] 214: orig. *rechristian*. [56] Thus also *Navire*. [57] 232: set, without apparent authority; 214: *you bet*. [58] 214: *tapping*. [59] 214: orig. *tipping*.
[60] 214: orig. *rise*. [61] 251: as here; 233: *polistaman*, in Joyce's hand; here as succeeding texts. [62] 214: set *waterloos* and altered as here. [63] 214: *Faith*. [64] 214: *Nemo*. [65] 214: altered orig. to *waiwhou in the annals*; then as here; for *waiwhou*, v. above. [66] 214: preceded by illegible strikeout. [67] 215: written over a word which is probably also *grainwaster*. [68] 215: r. edge of this page trimmed: –*ab* of *swab*, –*h* of *thrash*, and –*o* of second *to* conjectured. [69] 215: foll. by strikeout *for*.
[70] 215: orig. *sarthin* for bracketed passage; –*d* of *and* conjectured. [71] 215: *Bray*. [72] 215: *changes*. [73] 215: set *mind* and altered. [74] 215: set *between*. [75] 215: set *and Conn and Cullin* for bracketed passage. [76] 215: set *No, no, no and no!*; then *Neya, Naya, No and Naux!*; then *Neya, Narev, No and Naux!*. [77] Yale

* All page numbers refer to B. M. Add. MS 47474. The *transition* galleys are 209–225; the two sets of *transition* page proof are 227–246 and 248–257.

ANNA LIVIA PLURABELLE

copy: preceded by illegible strikeout. [78] 215: *dingley* altered to *dingling*. [79] Thus also *Navire*.
[80] *in the* to *listening* also in *Navire*. [81] 234: *his wrists* altered to *the pulse*; Yale copy: *the* (poss. *his*) *pulse* struck out in margin. [82] Thus also *Navire*. [83] Bracketed passage also in *Navire*. [84] 215: *kiss* altered to *kisokiss*. [85] Bracketed passage also in *Navire*; *–'s* without apparent authority; but thus *transition*. [86] Yale copy: foll. by illegible strikeout. [87] *–ic* conjectured. [88] *Navire*: *Naama is*. [89] 215: second *–e–* conjectured.
[90] 215: *Churruta*; *transition*: *Chirauta*, as both page proofs. [91] Thus also *transition*; but 252 corrects as here in Joyce's hand. [92] Thus also *transition*; but 252 corrects as here in Joyce's hand. [93] 216: foll. by strikeout *loathing*. [94] Thus also *transition*. [95] 216: *Monday* altered to *Sitterday*; Yale copy: illegible strikeout after *Munaday* in bracketed passage. [96] 216: set *material*; includes closing parenthesis. [97] [217]: set *in sub*. [98] [217]: *upside* altered to *tipside*, then as here; *hammam*, below, set *hamman* in *transition*; cf. succeeding texts. [99] 236: set off with commas in Joyce's hand; Yale copy: *bingkar* or *bingkan*; cf. Text F.
[100] [217]: orig. *By*. [101] [217]: foll. by strikeout *blessed*. [102] [217]: foll. by strikeout *she would*. [103] [217]: *don't be*. [104] [217]: *chapbooks*. [105] Thus *transition*; [217] omits. [106] [217]: set *pawn*. [107] Thus also *Navire*. [108] [219]: orig. *lippelets*. [109] [219]: orig. *violets*.
[110] [219]: set *Brie-on-Arrose*, as also *transition*; 253: altered as here, poss. by Joyce. [111] 237: set *sprizzling*, without apparent authority. [112] [219]: *orged*, in Joyce's hand; but v. succeeding texts. [113] [219]: *out of her basin* for preceding four words. [114] Thus also *Navire*. [115] [219]: orig. *Ishecrri* foll. by strikeout *or*. [116] [219]: *washe toney*. [117] [219]: *quaint*; 238: set *quirkint* (an obvious conflation); *transition* as here, without apparent authority. [118] [219]: orig. *on*; division of *ourthe* unavoidable. [119] 218: *lobs*.
[120] 218: *Listeners*. [121] 218: foll. by strikeout *her*. [122] 218: orig. *pocketsides*. [123] 218: orig. *wind*. [124] 218: set *fiuming* and altered as here. [125] Thus also *transition*, without apparent authority. [126] 218: *on the road* altered to *long the road*. [127] 218: *dowse*, as also *Navire*. [128] 218: *fruiteying*. [129] 254: poss. *anober*.
[130] 239: foll. by *Radile-me-rudall the restigouche* in Joyce's hand; but v. succeeding texts. [131] 239: altered to *wentworth*; but v. succeeding texts. [132] 220: *line*. [133] 220: set *curars* and altered to *curaro*. [134] 220: altered to *wich*, which is then struck out. [135] 220: orig. *weser*. [136] 220: *herself*. [137] Yale copy: preceded by strikeout, poss. *kall*. [138] 220: *bending*. [139] 220: orig. *and*.
[140] 220: foll. by strikeout *nos*. [141] 220: *gave*, preceded by strikeout *gave her*; the entire passage in double brackets is poss. intended to follow *pollynooties*, below. [142] 220: orig. *long live* for bracketed passage. [143] Thus also *Navire*. [144] Thus also *Navire*. [145] 240: set thus, without apparent authority. [146] Thus also *transition*. [147] 220: *Toucher Doyle* altered to *Toucher Thumb*; 207 (a corrigenda sheet) emends *Thumb* to *Thomb*; but *transition*: *Thumb*. [148] 221: orig. *Blanche's*. [149] 221: orig. *breeches*, then *breechies*.
[150] 221: *for*; 240: *to*, without apparent authority; but v. succeeding texts. [151] 221: *for*; 240: *to*, without apparent authority; but v. succeeding texts. [152] 221: orig. *in the* [153] 221: *morn*; 240 as here, without apparent authority. [154] Yale copy: orig. *Arruna*. [155] 207 (corrigenda sheet): emended here. [156] 221: this alteration written, deleted, and then rewritten. [157] *transition*: *Twimijim*. [158] 221: set *glory*, as on 207 (corrigenda sheet), which contains the entire passage in single brackets. [159] 221: *plenty*; Yale copy: poss. *panteplenty*; here as in succeeding texts.

NOTES

[160] 221: *lashings*. [161] 221: *Lona*. [162] 221: *breeks*, altered to *braggies*, then as here. [163] 221: orig. *Bella*. [164] Thus also *Navire*; *oakanknee*, below, is foll. in *transition* by an *a*. [165] *transition*: *Maggi*. [166] Bracketed passage on 207 (corrigenda sheet); *he* orig. *she*. [167] 222: *MacPeace* and for *MacPacem*. [168] 222: *Susy*. [169] 222: *MacCabe* altered to *MacCall*.

[170] 222: *lent*. [171] 222: set *snufler's*, altered to *snuffler's*, then as here. [172] 222: bracketed passage set *cracked divine* and altered as here; *transition*: *cracka dvine*. [173] 222: orig. *the*. [174] 222: set *Churchyard* and altered as here. [175] 223: *O*. [176] 223: set *you Miller* and altered to *your Miller*. [177] The passage from *chuckles* to *flossies* is extremely corrupt textually as set on 223. It is altered on 223 to read as here. [178] 223: foll. by strikeout *the*. [179] Thus also *Navire*.

[180] Thus also *Navire*. [181] 243: *Regen*. [182] Yale copy: preceded by strikeout, poss. *grey*. [183] Emendation on Yale copy only. [184] 223: *of Thy*; 243: altered to *Thaya*. [185] 223: altered to *sioulers*, which is then struck out. [186] 223: passage evolves *nine to hold* (–*d* trimmed) *to the fire* [*and*] (–*d* trimmed) *and* [*ten*] [*one*] [*one's the cold*] *this for the code*; brackets indicate strikeouts. [187] 223: persistent error in typescripts (v. Text C) corrected here. [188] *transition*: *Meaghere*. [189] 224: *loop*.

[190] Yale copy: poss. *Onimas*; but v. succeeding texts. [191] 224: *And*. [192] 224: *died* altered to *deed*. [193] 224: *died* altered to *deed*. [194] 224: *stuck*. [195] Thus also *Navire*. [196] 224: orig. *mouths*. [197] 224: set *clever* and altered here. [198] 224: *saw*; 224: *sa* (but page is frayed at edge). [199] 224: passage evolves [*We see the wonder*] *We see* [*the wonder's*] *that wonder in your eye*; brackets indicate strikeouts.

[200] 224: set *I see my chart* and altered to *My chart* [*on*] *shines high*; brackets indicate strikeout. [201] 224: set *take* for preceding two words and altered here. [202] 245: orig. *And safe* for preceding two words. [203] 224: *Tow will*, as also *Navire*. [204] *Navire*: *twinkletoes*; 224: *trinklytoes*; 245: as here, without apparent authority. [205] 225: final page of galley begins here and is numbered "33." [206] 225: *John Joe*, as *Navire*; 245, 257: *Joe John*, without apparent authority; but thus succeeding texts. [207] 225, 245: *the*; 257: set *oure*, without apparent authority; but thus succeeding texts. [208] 225, 245: *the*; 257 set *eure*, without apparent authority; but thus succeeding texts. [209] 225: upside down at the bottom of the page in Joyce's hand: "lapping a rise/time and tide." The proof is also marked "lu et approuvé/James Joyce/Paris/22 Octobre 1927." Yale copy signed: "James Joyce/Paris/2 February 1928."

Notes to Text F *

[1] 259: sentence emended so as to read *Wash away and quit be dabbling*; but succeeding texts as here. [2] 259: orig. *Mixing*. [3] 259: orig. *Droched*. [4] 259: *wrong*. [5] 260: set *codfish*; altered to *codfisk*; then as here. [6] 260: set *phwat*; presumed alteration on postulated galleys; cf. Text E and note. [7] 260: set *coxyt'* and altered; but cf. Text E; succeeding texts as here. [8] Thus Faber, without apparent authority. [9] 260: *dam* inserted to follow and then struck out.

[10] 260: pn. thus, in Joyce's hand; *see how* in preceding phrase of Text E crossed out on 212. [11] 260: omits. [12] 260: *dochther*; but succeeding texts as here. [13] Thus succeeding texts; but possibly a reversion; cf. Text E. [14] 261: *sorgue*. [15] Both ALPS omit. [16] Thus Faber, without apparent authority. [17] 262: *by wan by wan* for preceding two words; Gaige: *bywanbywan*; Faber, as here.

* All page numbers refer to B. M. Add. MS 47474.

109

ANNA LIVIA PLURABELLE

[18] The sheet containing the germ of this addition is in the Lockwood Memorial Library at the University of Buffalo. [19] 262: foll. by strikeout *aimai aim*.
[20] Thus 262 and succeeding texts, without apparent authority. [21] 262: *jumnped*, altered to *jumnpad*; Gaige: *jumnpad*. [22] 262: *silvamoonlike* appears to be written over the text as given; but succeeding texts as here. [23] 262: set thus, without apparent authority; but thus also succeeding texts. [24] 263: foll. by strikeout *gab*; both ALPS *A froth-dizzying*. [25] 263: orig. *high*. [26] Gaige: *picts*. [27] 263: Thus, without apparent authority; but thus also succeeding texts. [28] 264: orig. *Hoo*, then *Howl* or *How'l*. [29] 264: *Axe*.

[30] 265: altered to read *turfentie*; but succeeding texts as here. [31] 265: *rhinestones* altered to *rhunerhinestones*. [32] Thus 265 and succeeding texts, without apparent authority. [33] Gaige: *ladyfair* for preceding two words. [34] 266: *all aflume* added here, but omitted from succeeding texts. [35] Thus 266 and succeeding texts, without apparent authority. [36] 266: orig. *southsides*. [37] 266 and Gaige: *wich*; v. Text E and note. [38] 267: orig. *doors*. [39] 267: foll. by strikeouts *bau* and *bei*.

[40] 267: foll. by strikeout *too*. [41] 267: orig. *aflood*. [42] 267: *Anna* altered to *Anno*; but succeeding texts as here. [43] 267: *recorder*. [44] 268 and Gaige: *tolast* for preceding two words. [45] 268 and Gaige: aC_3. [46] 268: strikeout *sw* appears here also. [47] 268: set foll. by *and*; cf. Text E. [48] 269: possibly intended to be struck out. [49] 269: set thus without apparent authority; but thus also succeeding texts.

[50] 269: *cracka*, as Yale copy; but cf. Text E and note; succeeding texts as here. [51] Faber italicizes as FW in remainder of sentence. [52] 270: *anyone* altered to *erewon*. [53] 270: *Sexaloiter*. [54] 271: *Greekoroman*, foll. by *when*. [55] 271: *but*. [56] 271 has a blank space here. [57] 271: *disagree*. [58] 271: *vericoarse*. [59] 271: *the blind* for bracketed passage.

[60] See also note on FW, 203.23, in *Textual Appendix*.

BIBLIOGRAPHICAL NOTE

For a bibliography of texts of translations, which are not taken account of in this edition, see John J. Slocum and Herbert Cahoon's *A Bibliography of James Joyce: 1882–1941* (New Haven, 1953). Among the translations, the French and the Basic English are of most interest.

For an extensive explication of the entire chapter, see my unpublished University of Minnesota dissertation, "James Joyce's Revisions of *Finnegans Wake*: A Study of the Published Versions." Other explications of particular passages may be found in Walton Litz, "The Evolution of Joyce's *Anna Livia Plurabelle*," *PhilQ*, XXXVI (1957), 36–48, and in John Hinsdale Thompson's notes to the final paragraphs of the chapter in Kimon Friar and John Malcolm Brinnin's *Modern Poetry: British and American* (New York, 1951).

For comments on the chapter as a whole, see Padraic Colum's "Preface" to the Gaige edition (not reprinted in the Faber edition), Robert Sage's essay in *Our Exagmination*, Edmund Wilson's *Axel's Castle*, and the standard works of Kenner, Levin, and Tindall. There is pertinent discussion also in the following:

Cope, Jackson I.: "James Joyce: Test Case for a Theory of Style." *ELH*, XXI (1954), 221–236.

Dolmatch, Theodore B.: "Notes and Queries Concerning the Revisions of *FW*." *MLQ*, XVI (1955), 142–148.

Hill, Archibald A.: "A Philologist Looks at *FW*." *VQR*, XV (1939), 650–656.

Hodgart, M. J. C.: "The Earliest Sections of *FW*." *JJR*, I (1957), 3–18.

In addition to the sources above, Richard Ellmann's *James Joyce* (New York, 1959) may be consulted for additional details of composition. And M. J. C. Hodgart and Mabel Worthington's *Song in the Works of James Joyce* (New York, 1959) lists the unidentified song of the paragraph analyzed in the "Introduction."

www.ingramcontent.com/pod-product-compliance
Lightning Source LLC
Chambersburg PA
CBHW061419300426
44114CB00015B/1991